Popular Culture, Piracy, and Outlaw Pedagogy

Youth, Media, & Culture Series
Volume 01

Series Editor:
Shirley R. Steinberg, *University of Calgary, Canada*

Editorial Board

Giuliana Cucinelli, *Concordia University, Montreal*
Rhonda Hammer, *UCLA, USA*
Mark Helmsing, *Michigan State University, USA*
Brian Johnson, *Bloomburg University, PA, USA*
Pepi Leistyna, *University of Massachusetts, Boston, USA*

Scope

Taking the notion of critical youth studies, this series features top scholars in critical media and youth studies. Coupling edgy topics with a critical theoretical lens, volumes explore the impact of media and culture on youth....and the impact of youth on media and culture.

Popular Culture, Piracy, and Outlaw Pedagogy

A Critique of the Miseducation of Davy Jones

Elizabeth Alford Pollock
Independent Scholar

SENSE PUBLISHERS
ROTTERDAM/BOSTON/TAIPEI

A C.I.P. record for this book is available from the Library of Congress.

ISBN: 978-94-6209-611-0 (paperback)
ISBN: 978-94-6209-612-7 (hardback)
ISBN: 978-94-6209-613-4 (e-book)

Published by: Sense Publishers,
P.O. Box 21858,
3001 AW Rotterdam,
The Netherlands
https://www.sensepublishers.com/

Printed on acid-free paper

For Tommy, Emily, and Abby
And for all those teachers who have the courage to embrace the pirate within.

TABLE OF CONTENTS

ACKNOWLEDGEMENTS

Every research project brings new opportunities to learn, yet that learning is unable to grow feet and move on its own without the complicated conversation William Pinar believes is crucial to the curricular process. If it were not for countless lunch dates with Pat Faulkner and Jill Roy, my ideas, concerns, and conjectures may have never reached the printed page.

I also thank Tommy, Emily, and Abby Pollock who supported me through love and knowing when to leave the house so I could complicate alone with only my thoughts. No project is worthwhile without you three in my life to share it with, along with Wesley and Faye Alford, Denise Coughenour, Diane Guthrie, and the rest of my growing family. Gail Pollock, my mother-in-law and musical artist extraordinaire, was influential in proofreading my work and informing me-brutally at times-when an idea lacked coherence. Thank you for being honest.

Finally, I would like to thank Bill Reynolds and series editor Shirley Steinberg for believing in the possibilities my manuscript affords. Bill became an avid supporter of my ideas early in the research process and repeatedly checked on my progress. Without his support, this text may have been pushed aside to be buried under tomorrow's urgent demands. I am very fortunate to have such wonderful people to call friends and family, and that is all a pirate needs.

PIRATES AS TREASURE CHESTS OF CURRICULAR EXPERIENCES

DISCOVERING THE TREASURE

I am not sure when it happened- the transition from childhood pirate curiosities to outright obsession was a slow process. Like many children reared under the influence of Disney Imagineering, I grew up with Peter Pan, Wendy, and the Lost Boys. We hid from Captain Hook in trees, behind bushes, and sometimes in the creek that ran through my backyard. As time evolved from childhood to my teenage years, the Lost Boys were replaced by living peers who provided more entertainment than my imaginary friends of long ago. But I never escaped the feeling that pirates were trying to teach me something; there was more to their story than hooked hands, eye patches, or pegged legs.

My curiosity peaked again in high school while reading Stevenson's *Treasure Island*, and then again with the release of Tri-Star Picture's cinematic adaptation of *Hook* in 1991. These moments would take me back to my backyard and my childhood hideouts where I felt safe behind the bushes, beyond the clutches of Captain Hook. But it wasn't until I met Jack Sparrow and Davy Jones that my curiosities developed new meanings. By this time, I had two children of my own, and they had petitioned to have a movie-watching marathon, wanting to view the *Pirates of the Caribbean* trilogy in one sitting. It was cold, raining, and no other activities presented themselves so we embarked on what we called our "pirate expedition." Of course, once the infamous Davy Jones commandeered the screen, my children scattered like the wind, abandoning me with only my thoughts.

Jack Sparrow's image as the honorable pirate juxtaposed next to a corrupt and mutated Davy Jones appeared to be a little *too* scripted for my taste, and the blaring dichotomy rekindled questions from my childhood relating to what pirates were attempting to instruct. Smith, Smith, and Watkins suggest "pop culture crosses time and also changes with time since pop culture icons can disappear as quickly as they become popular, return with a wave of nostalgia, or stay around for decades" (2009, p. 4). Pirates in popular culture have a tendency to ride these cultural shifts of time, fading away into rose-tinted memories only to re-emerge again to recapture the imagination of a new generation of youngsters. Perhaps nostalgia is what has kept pirates alive since the height of their escapades in the early 1700's- I do not know; whatever the reasons, the image of the pirate has remained relatively stable.

My first question regarding the juxtaposition of Sparrow/Jones in relation to the stability of the pirate image over time was "why," meaning, was there some sort of cultural benefit in perpetuating these stable significations? *Pirates of the Caribbean* certainly embraced the stereotypes in the characterizations of Ragetti with his eye patch in *At World's End*, Sailor Cotton with his parrot, trained to speak for him as he had no tongue and present in all three films, and Captain Barbossa with the peg-leg he adorned for *On Stranger Tides* - the fourth installment of the pirate films and not discussed in this text. There appeared to be an underlying master narrative scripting what culture - popular and otherwise - teaches regarding the pirate. Steeped in postmodern theory, my thoughts began to hoist their own colours, raise the proverbial black flag, and I began to question these narratives.

Lyotard teaches:

> The popular stories themselves recount what could be called positive or negative apprenticeships...in other words, the successes and failures greeting the hero's undertakings: These successes or failures either bestow legitimacy upon social institutions (the function of myths), or represent positive or negative models (the successful or unsuccessful hero) of integration into established institutions (legends and tales). (1979, pp. 19-20)

Jack Sparrow is the unsung hero in the pirate films with the antagonist shifting from Captain Barbossa in *Curse of the Black Pearl* to Davy Jones in *Dead Man's Chest* to Lord Cutler Beckett in *At World's End*. Throughout each story, Sparrow's heroic image is tested as he faces one moral dilemma after another. Through his trials and tribulations, I questioned what institutions or ideologies he and other characters were legitimizing. Whatever they were, the pirate films make explicit the slippery slope dividing Sparrow/Jones was a process one engaged to *become* a delegitimized Other; a conscious choice one makes for one's self. The process itself reflected a narrative of privilege contradicting historical images of pirates as second-class citizens-pirates had no privileges in society. Some pirates did make the choice to enter the world of piracy, but this choice was influenced by the lack of opportunities they had available while on land. Some pirates were press-ganged onto ships and forced to sail under the black flag, but they faced the gallows unless they could substantiate their impressments with circumstantial evidence. This evidence was rarely enough to sway a jury of their peers which had already condemned pirates to death upon acknowledgement of the pirate label. After all, in a pirate's world, you were guilty until proven innocent.

When I began the daunting task of researching pirate history (for there are literally hundreds of texts in pirate culture and cultural studies), I came to understand that the binaries employed in *Pirates of the Caribbean* were an extension of a dichotomy constructed in seventeenth century culture and society between a privateer (read legal) and a pirate (read illegal). What became apparent through these constructions was the struggle between power and resistance. Pirates not only resisted the colonization of their ships, they rejected being defined by imperialism and a social hierarchy through which they rarely benefitted. Of course, that did not stop them from bringing these codifications onto the ships themselves through their own

2

language and cultures. In so doing, they inadvertently assisted in the construction of the need to be re-presented as the piratical Other to the privateer, which cultural and governmental institutions had already legitimized through pirate actions.

What also became evident was how these historical and popular representations have worked to benefit a neoliberal ideology with traces of corporate allegiance dating back to the Golden Age, leading up to twenty-first century representations of the pirates of Somalia. I find no coincidence that the height of pirate activities in the 1700's paralleled with the height of expansion via the East India Company's imperial reign of terror on India, other regions involved in maritime trade such as China, and also the height of British colonization. While other Empires existed during this time period such as the Spanish and the Portuguese, the pirates of the Golden Age, at least the ones written about, tended to be of European descent. And the Golden Age marked a time of birth for pirate history and popular cultural images of the stereotypes we live with today.

READING THE TREASURE MAP

As a result of historical struggles between pirates and the forces of imperialism and colonialism, I also came to recognize the history of pirates as a history of people, with the interconnections between power and resistance in effect today acting mimetically to the interconnections between power and resistance operating during the Golden Age. The pirates' curriculum explored in this text traverses the boundaries of the historical struggle between imperial powers and pirate resistance. This struggle points towards potential new directions for the field of Curriculum Studies in relation to our own struggles with boundaries imposed by neoliberal ideologies working to delegitimize teachers and public education for the benefit of privatization.

Since the field of Curriculum Studies has been relatively silent on the subject of pirates, it is necessary to present a historiography of their struggles and the relationship pirate representations have within the limited neoliberal framings of their experiences. Chapter One explores the language constructing early representations leading up to present images we have of the pirate while introducing the frameworks of postmodern and postcolonial theory to question this language. By drawing on Derridian interpretations of the *pharmakon*, I am able to introduce what has been consistently absent in pirate cultural debates: the absence of the trace of the verb *pirao* and its meaning of "getting experience."

Chapter Two focuses on the historiography of pirates from a postmodern lens while engaging various arguments for and against the possibilities a postmodern perspective offers. By juxtaposing this historiography next to the images and language represented in *Pirates of the Caribbean*, its neoliberal ideology becomes evident as it works to limit individual interpretations of freedom. Chapter Three engages a postcolonial perspective, offering a historiography of imperialism, colonialism, and the effects a British East India Company had both on a colonized

India and the pirates in general. This history is also juxtaposed next to the images and language represented in *Pirates of the Caribbean*, and the imperial codifications embedded within contemporary systems of language are opened.

Weaver and Daspit argue "popular culture texts offers a pedagogy of possibility in which societal problems are addressed [and] silenced voices heard" (2000, xxvii). Chapter Four marks a shift in my writing by employing the historiography of pirates and the external forces applied by British colonization and imperial East India Companies presented in previous chapters as a framework for questioning how the pirates of Somalia are represented within cultural spaces. In effort to create a location for the silenced voices of Somalia to be heard, I draw on references interacting directly with pirates such as an interview conducted by Jay Bahadur in *The Pirates of Somalia* (2011) and also the interviews and quotations of Somali citizens such as rap artist K'Naan and those who identify with the pirate label. By exploring the conditions of pirate resurgence, the struggle between power and resistance re-activating itself in twenty-first century culture becomes evident.

While working on the first four chapters, my mind kept conjuring up images of historical pirates, the characters in *Pirates of the Caribbean*, and contemporary pirates, all positioned in chronological order. I began to sketch these images in my journal: elaborate displays of stick people with elongated swords, triangular hats perched atop their perfectly round heads, and the best interpretation of a feather I could muster, protruding at unequal intervals from each pirate's hat. All of them were perched atop a half-moon shaped vessel with wavy lines symbolizing water. I did not notice initially, but as the sketches evolved, I had begun to insert rectangular-shaped buildings in the background, oblivious of the illogic involved in picturing buildings floating on the sea. But once my eyes fixated on the image, I recognized that the one thread weaving throughout the three sets of pirates was the image of the corporation run amok, a more logical conclusion when one views current corporate activities as the modus operandi of contemporary interpretations of imperialism. Ideologies are versatile, traveling to any and all places in the world. During the Golden Age, there was the ruthless behavior of individuals on behalf of the East India Company, with the pirate films reinforcing this image. But as I toyed with the chronology of the pictures, repositioning the present as the past, I realized the modern day actions and interpretations of the corporation appeared to be reliving the brutality and callous disregard to human life displayed during the Golden Age of Piracy. The real treasure being sought was not some fabled interpretation of Aztec Gold as in *Curse of the Black Pearl*, but the hearts of the people constructing contemporary culture and society within the U.S. and abroad- i.e. the hearts of you and me.

Of course, this was only a picture. I needed a perspective articulating the image I had already drawn. The image was the key to unlocking the secrets embedded within *Pirates of the Caribbean*. I found what I was looking for in Gasset's *Revolt of the Masses*. When I reviewed the pirate trilogy through the eyes of Gasset, the picture I had sketched began to reveal itself in words. Chapter Five presents this image by exploring how the brutality embraced by the characters in the pirate films emulates

4

the brutality on display in contemporary cultural contexts at the hands of individuals reflecting Gasset's characterization of the mass man. In order to understand the context in which a contemporary revolt of the masses may occur, I engage the use of a conjecture, positing a "what if" scenario by positioning the corporation personified by the U.S. Supreme Court to fill the role of Gasset's hypothetical mass man. Included in this chapter is an explanation as to how Gasset defines his concept of the mass man as well as how I define the corporation. In so doing, I am able to view the shape of empire's structural violence as a set of catachrestic boundaries impressing on every facet of our lives. This brutal structure is where we, as teachers and as human beings, are presently situated.

Continuing the conjecture initiated in chapter Five, chapter Six situates the teacher in between the pirate and the hypothetical mass man to explore how imperialism and the corporation's desire to capture our hearts induces an existential crisis experienced when caught in between these two worlds: a crisis leading to the potential revolt Gasset depicts in his text.

Here is where the Sparrow/Jones dichotomy collapses into itself, symbolizing the weakest point of the mass man's DNA but the strongest point in ours. Here is where we may counter the brutality we are witnessing at the hands of the mass man with the radical love and will to power pirates reflected in their individual and collective actions. In so doing, the miseducation of Davy Jones is revealed and, should we choose to learn from this, Jones's miseducation may become an experience we bring with us to all future readings of the world in hopes of thwarting the miseducational process.

Chapter Seven applies the lessons learned from a pirates' curriculum by offering Outlaw Pedagogy as both a pedagogy of possibilities Daspit and Weaver argue are necessary for interpreting popular culture texts, and also a pedagogy of passion and purpose reflected in the lived experiences of historical pirates such as Bartholomew Roberts and one of the greatest educators of our time, Paulo Freire. It is my hope this text contributes to the "complicated conversation" Pinar (2004) believes is crucial to understanding curriculum. In so doing, we expand the circle of catachrestic boundaries imposed on us through language systems, learn to pirate moments of authentic learning for ourselves and our students, and contest the limitations imposed on our spaces through neoliberal ideologies shrouding schools today. Whereas Davy Jones literally had no heart in the films, both Roberts and Freire teach us that a *Pedagogy of the Heart* (Freire, 1997) is our best recourse as teachers. By re-engaging the heart in educational settings, we may learn to embrace the pirate we always already are.

LIMITATIONS TO THE TEXT

There are some limitations to the text I wish to acknowledge as they frame my account of piratical experiences. For starters, piracy has historically been considered "a man's world." While there were female pirates such as Anne Bonny and Mary

Read operating during the Golden Age, our understanding of their experiences was written by a male Captain Johnson. Contemporary accounts offer no exception to the patriarchal view of the pirate. Most of the narratives emerging out or on behalf of Somalia are still penned by masculine hands. While I do offer a challenge to this perspective in chapter Four, the historiography presented in the first three chapters utilizes the masculine pronoun to reflect the patriarchy embedded within both European and colonial (U.S.) culture during that time period. Once the challenge presents itself, the male phenomenon we call piracy is opened to include the female pronoun which I embody.

The second limitation deals with my representation of Somali pirates. Throughout the chapter addressing pirate resurgence, I struggled with the possibility that my own Western situatedness would add to the silencing of Somali voices rather than carving a space for their voices to be heard, or would contribute to Western re-presentations delegitimizing potential reasons for pirate resurgence. I take my lead from Marla Morris. While researching the events at Auschwitz and the Holocaust, Morris recognized her limits to knowing the events first-hand as these were not experiences she had actually lived. Even reading the accounts of the terror that constructed Auschwitz could not completely relay the horror of the past. Yet she tells us, "If we refuse the call of remembering this event altogether because of the ineffableness of Auschwitz, we lapse back into silence. Silence kills" (2001, p. 6). I wish not to add to the death of Somali voices in my struggle to understand their plight. So my own situatedness inside the Western perspective becomes my limit to knowing. It is the boundary which seeks to divide me from
Somali voices, reinforced by the geographical and cultural distance we share.

I have already discussed the employment of first-hand accounts emerging out of Somalia to address this limitation. I also focus my attention on how the West re-presents Somali pirates in order to open the dialogue to questions, such as, who benefits from such re-presentations? Who pays the cost? In so doing, I am able to understand how their silencing parallels to contemporary constructs of K-12 teachers and how the corporation of the past appears to have doubled its efforts to further silence the voices of a population of people desperate to be heard; the delicate dance between power and resistance reinserts itself into culture and society. These are the limitations constructing my reading of the pirate. It is my hope that by understanding these limits to knowing, I may teach others that pirates were much more than the tyrants of long ago. They were also human.

CHAPTER 1

ON BEING/BECOMING A PIRATE

CONSTRUCTING AN IMAGE

Imagine if you will a circle massive in construction and over three hundred years in the making. We are sitting inside this circle, you and I. You may not yet see its construction, but I do. Curve-shaped bookcases assemble three-fourths of its circumference, extending upwards as far as the eyes can see. Volumes upon volumes of leather-bound texts adorn the shelves. The folds in their bindings reflect centuries of engagement and use by their patrons. Each bookcase is erected out of mahogany posts, providing a structure for much of what have been written. One cannot help but feel engulfed by this knowledge, where Coleridge's *Rime of the Ancient Mariner* sits comfortably next to *Lempriere's Dictionary*- the age difference is vast.

The remaining fourth houses a fireplace with flames barely escaping the lids of the logs as they fight to sleep. A wrought-iron fire poker leans effortlessly against the fireplace's mahogany encasement. Above the mantle stands a large map of the West, overbearing in its presence both in the map itself and in the influence over many of the ideas set forth in the literature present. On each side of the map, sextants are cast aside by technological advances, honorably refusing to relinquish their importance in maritime history.

The center of the room is canvassed with tapestry rugs, hiding the wear of travelers past. Several wooden tables are positioned at random, with brown high back leather chairs anchoring each end. There are others in the room but they do not see us. A teacher is sitting in one of the chairs, attempting to call roll, it seems, and trying desperately to capture the attention of the others.

"Henry," she says, "William, are you here?"

"*Aye*," claims the man with his back to her. She cannot see him, but he is making faces at the others. They are lying on the tables.

"*Edward, please pay attention*," she says to the man whose presence cast an eerie shadow over the others.

"John, that leaves you. John?"

"*I'm here*," retorts a man whose existence has been influential in the cultural construction of his kind. They, too, are sitting on top of the tables. All except Jack, who is sitting in a boxcar; the kind you find on a roller coaster. A rowdy bunch to say the least and one whose presence has stirred the imagination of many who have read of their adventures. Two women are accounted for, Anne and Mary, but they are on another table, set apart from the others and conversing quietly amongst themselves. A few spaces beyond this motley crew stands Derrida, at a distance, mixing something in mortars and pestles. At first glance, he appears strangely out of place. But then again, wasn't it Derrida who warned us to be mindful of what first hides itself from view? Curiosity gets the best of us and we begin to walk in his direction. We are ready to speak with him through his writing, approaching with caution. But just as we are within reach, enormous crab-like claws grab hold of our being, nearly crushing us as they thrust us down a desolate black hole...to nothing. We are caught inside the abyss known as Davy Jones's locker. But we never reach the bottom. We are caught in between. We hear Jones's voice vibrating down the shaft:

"Tell me," he says, "do you get the picture?"

Laughing, I say to no one, "yes, I get the picture," and my eyes open once more to the recurring image I have envisioned for months. During that time, I have deliberated on whether to begin a writing project with such an ill-conceived fiction, but Derrida convinced me. Derrida believed the reader held a certain degree of responsibility to the text. "One must manage," he argues, "to think this out" (1981, p. 63); "this" being whatever is first hidden from the reader; "the hidden thread," as Derrida phrased it. What is hidden in my own introduction is why Derrida *belongs* in an image constructed of pirates. But to understand what is hiding, I first had to provide you with the image, even when there is no guarantee that what you constructed through your reading is the same image I intended to construct through my writing. So again, forgive me, and let us do as Derrida instructs; that is, "let us begin again" (1981, p. 3).

READING THE IMAGE

Hopefully, the first reading generated some questions for us to ponder. The most obvious being how we knew the characters in the room were pirates. Quite simply, I told you. Because history has delegated pirates to outlaw status, the study of these ancient mariners is relegated mainly to pirate lore, popular culture, or specific literary pursuit. Unless you know the socially constructed fables of the past, you may have missed this nod to their identification. When the teacher was calling roll, she announced the presence of Henry, William, John and Edward. These are none other than the Captains Henry Morgan and William Kidd, both famous for their relationship with British Parliament; the former a legendary buccaneer so beloved by his fellow citizens of a Caribbean Island he was afforded Knighthood status by the Kings Court of Jamaica; the latter famous for his burying of gold and silver, thus giving birth to the myth of pirates burying their plunder on exotic islands as this was actually not standard practice. Most pirates spent their loot as soon as they reached port. For those who didn't, they rarely let it out of their sight. Captain Kidd was granted a commission by British Parliament to embark on a privateering mission in the Indian Ocean but was betrayed by a supporter and ultimately tried and hanged as a pirate, to which he never conceded.

John's birth name was Long John Silver and was delivered to us via the literary genius of Robert Louis Stevenson (1993/1905). Stevenson is credited with the popular cultural construction of pirates with wooden legs, parrots on their shoulders, buried treasure, and maps with big red X's marking the spot where this treasure could be found. Because of his meticulous attention to the details surrounding actual pirate adventurers such as the Captains Morgan and Kidd, Stevenson was able to construct an image that popularized these attributes and heroicized maritime villains, a construction in existence to this day. As a result, Long John Silver became a more famous pirate than any who literally sailed the seas. All except one: Edward Teach. Teach, however, was no fiction. His accounts were recorded by a handful of merchant sailors who lived to write of their encounters. One such account was recorded by Henry Bostock on December 5, 1717 describing "a tall spare man with a very black beard which he wore very long" (as quoted in Cordingly, 1996, p. 13). This description was embellished as the legendary status outlived the actual life of the man who came to be known as Blackbeard.

Captain Charles Johnson recorded Blackbeard's appearance as such:

> This beard was black, which he suffered to grow of an extravagant Length; as to Breadth, it came up to his eyes; he was accustomed to twist it with Ribbons, in small Tails...and turn them about his Ears...and stuck lighted Matches under his Hat, which appearing on each Side of his Face, his Eyes naturally looking fierce and wild, made him altogether such a Figure, that Imagination cannot form an Idea of a Fury, from Hell, to look more frightful. (Defoe, 1999/1972, pp. 84-85)

One may be so inclined as to think Blackbeard a myth if it weren't for the accounts of Bostock, Robert Maynard, who led the attack against Blackbeard ending his life, and logbook entries of the HMS *Lyme*, the HMS *Pearl*, and others (Cordingly, 1996).

Captain Johnson's text, *A General History of the Robberies and Murders of the Most Notorious Pyrates,* chronicles the events of Blackbeard and others associated with the "Golden Age of Piracy," dating from 1716-1726. Johnson includes the adventures of Anne Bonny and Mary Read, the only two women afforded pirate status, largely due to their inclusion in Johnson's text. Here we see a blurring of the boundaries between fact and fiction in that the histories of these two women became less about their own personal experiences and more about Johnson's *account* of these women. Both sailed under the command of a lesser-known pirate named Calico Jack. But this is not the Jack sitting in a car in the image I constructed. That particular Jack is the newly-famed maritime hero Jack Sparrow, born of the minds of Disney Imagineers who needed a character to embellish a theme park ride. This birth is precisely why Jack could not be found lying on a table in my image as his umbilical cord was not directly attached to a specific historical or fictional text. Thus, as the others were lying on the tables, they were, in fact, or in fiction, depending on your perspective, resting between the words, past and present tenses, and prepositional phrases one associates with language. They were, in fact, books. I have little doubt these literary pieces influenced the construction of Jack Sparrow as Calico Jack is depicted as a "reckless character whose colorful clothes had earned him the nickname" (Cordingly, 1996, p. 57), but one cannot know for certain. And Jack Sparrow's image, if anything, portrays the recklessness associated with Calico Jack.

This blurring of the boundaries between fact and fiction is precisely why a study of a pirate's curriculum must be conducted, so that we may explore this construction whose curriculum is taught predominately within popular cultural spaces. Thus, one of the posts constructing the bookshelves, symbolically "holding up" knowledge only to disrupt this structure, is postmodernism. As Pinar, Reynolds, Slattery and Taubman suggest, "The postmodern answer suggests there is an increasing awareness that there are only fantasies, fictions, versions of reality which claim to represent nothing but themselves" (1995, pp. 470-471). This statement is evidenced in how we in contemporary society approach the concept of pirate: as a thief, a robber, or, at a minimum, a questionable member of society.

Pinar's *et al.* statement is further evidenced in the controversy surrounding Captain Johnson. Considered the premier text on pirate history first published in 1724, Johnson relied on letters and Naval logbooks, trial documents, government reports, and depositions of both captured pirates and their victims to construct his *General History of Pyrates* (Cordingly, 1996). There has been little debate as to the validity of his claims. His text represents a personal relationship with the events unfolding at that time, and they further represent a person who was both well-traveled and well-connected with agencies associated with the adjudication of pirate crimes.

What *has* been debated since Johnson's publication was who Captain Johnson actually was. Outside of the *General History of Pyrates*, there is no evidence to suggest a Captain Johnson ever existed. There is no mention of a Captain Johnson in seaman's journals, naval logbooks or any traditional mode of record-keeping during that time period. There existed a persistent rumor that he was the playwright Charles Johnson who wrote *The Successful Pyrate* in 1812, but, according to Cindy Vallar and other websites addressing the mystery, that rumor was highly unlikely as the playwright publically rebuffed the fame associated with the text (2010, website). This left Johnson's identity to fanciful speculation for centuries.

Then, in 1932, American Scholar John Robert Moore presented a theory that Johnson was none other than celebrated writer Daniel Defoe, famous for his authoring of *Robinson Crusoe* and *Captain Singleton* (Cordingly, 1996; see also Parry, 2006). Moore compared the literary styles of Johnson and Defoe, the travels and connections both men are believed to have shared, and a fascination with pirates Defoe was reported to have embodied. His conclusion was that Defoe *had to be* the enigmatic Captain Johnson. Moore's argument was so convincing during that time period many scholars began to cite Defoe instead of Johnson in their work. Indeed, the copy of the *General History of Pyrates* I draw on for my research is authored by Defoe, but I have no way for knowing for certain. I give credence to the name on the text before me, but I do not know whose ideas I am perpetuating in my own epistemological pursuit.

To complicate matters, in 1988, Moore's theory was "demolished," as Cordingly articulates, by two scholars who argued there "was not a single piece of documentary evidence to link Defoe with *The General History of Pyrates*" (1996, xx) and focused their attention on the discrepancies between this particular text and Defoe's other work. Since this time, the authorship of the text in question has been returned to Captain Johnson. But that still leaves open the question of Johnson's identity and may very well be the greatest mystery of all emerging out of this time period.

The debates, questions, and historical fact or fictional accounts of the Golden Age of Piracy are reflected in the map of the West in the image I constructed. A World Map is also embedded within the text of *Pirates of the Caribbean, At World's End* (2007). This map is viewed in one of the opening scenes of the film as it is initially being painted. Throughout the movie, the painter is seen working towards completion, when, in one of the final scenes, the map is finally finished. The antagonist in *At World's End* is Lord Cutler Beckett. Representing the operations of the East India Trading Company and its relationship with British Parliament, Beckett also sees the completion of his dream to seize total control over global waters once all pirates have been eradicated from the seas. The map's completion symbolizes this conquest. I, however, include the map for a very different reason. I argue the interpretation of pirate is itself a Western construction, built out of the need to delegitimize an entire sect of people who were deemed outside of what it meant to be a good and productive citizen. In this process, another group of people, privateers, were afforded legitimacy by both British and Spanish Parliaments and the "commoners" who inhabited both land and sea, when many of the actions and behaviors of privateers were actually no different than pirates.

David Cordingly distinguishes between pirates and privateers via a "Letter of Marque" privateers were afforded by the King: of England, of Spain, for example. This letter granted independent sailors reprisal against those who were deemed enemies of the King, with varying proportions of goods accumulated during an expedition shared between the King, ship owners, the Captain and his crew. Pirates did not possess such letters. Cordingly states, "In theory, an authorized privateer was recognized by international law and could not be prosecuted for piracy, but the system was wide open to abuse and privateers were often no more than licensed pirates" (1996, xvii-xviii). The murky waters existing between these two terms are exactly how Captain Kidd was tried and hanged for piracy. Having taken advantage of the ability to raid ships of their riches, Kidd seized the *Quedah Merchant's* cargo yet failed to arrest its Captain. When word of his actions reached port- along with rumors of his other escapades- Kidd sought refuge in both Long Island and his business partner, Lord Bellemont, now Governor of New York, who was entangled in his own political game. In an effort to distance his actions from Kidd's to protect his own reputation, Bellemont called for Kidd to be placed on trial for piracy.

Now, according to Dan Parry, "since the idea of stepping beyond the law was largely dismissed by privateers, it is a mistake to think of them as simply 'legalized pirates'" (2006, p. 38). Yet Captain Kidd never conceded his acts as piracy as he viewed these acts well within the realm of the law. He did not have to. Others seeking to protect their own political ambitions such as Bellemont afforded Kidd the pirate label in an effort to delegitimize Kidd while further securing his own legitimacy in the eyes of his constituents.

The experience of Captain Kidd demonstrates how our knowledge of pirates is due largely to how others depicted these individuals as few pirates kept journals of their travels. I contend the construction of pirates is emblematic of Edward Said's *Orientalism*. Said argued Orientalism was less about actual cultural and societal practices of those inhabiting the Orient and more about how the West constructed the *image* of the Orient in its place (1979). Likewise, the cultural construction of pirate as a murderous, treasure-hunting villain with no morals and distinct from privateers is also a Western construction embellished by three hundred years of fiction, film, and legend which have converged to construct our image of these outlaws. The map of the Western hemisphere reflects this cultural construction with Said serving as the original artist to the ideas perpetuated in my work. Therefore, not only is Said's presence felt in the map, but also in another post I draw on to construct my theoretical framework, that of postcolonialism.

Another scholar associated with postcolonialism is Gayatri Spivak. Of particular interest is her interpretation of the catachresis. Spivak instructs:

> Within the historical frame of exploration, colonization, decolonization- what is being effectively reclaimed is a series of regulative political concepts, the *supposedly* authoritative narrative of the production of which was written elsewhere...They are being reclaimed, indeed claimed, as concept-metaphors for which no historically adequate referent may be advanced from postcolonial space, yet that does not make the claims less important. A concept-metaphor without an adequate referent is a catachresis. (1993, p. 67, emphasis in original)

Indeed, there is no concept-metaphor existing outside of a language system in which we are born, and which we perpetuate daily through our teaching and interacting with others. Yet, because we are immersed in this language, we are often blind to other interpretations beyond that which dominates the conversation. The catachresis is not necessarily a place we wish to inhabit, but we have no way of escaping (Spivak, 1993; Coloma, Means, & Kim, 2009). This symbolizes, not only my own predicament in relation to Jones and the clutch he currently holds on my being for which I can escape, but also in the interpretation of what it *potentially means to be a pirate,* for which no exodus is available.

DERRIDA...A PIRATE?

The above statement provides an entry into what may be the other prevailing question of my image. Why does Derrida belong in an image full of pirates? The answer to this question rests in Derrida's actions. Derrida was not just mixing *something.* Rather, he was mixing words and interpretations in an effort to demonstrate how these words always carry multiple meanings, and how these words also rest on a fabled desire to oppose an Other through their own construction. Nowhere is this more evident than in Derrida's interpretation of the *pharmakon*. The *pharmakon*, the written text, acts as a drug that both remedies and poisons the body. Therefore, any inscription of the *pharmakon* necessarily inscribes two possible meanings that both oppose and support each other (1981). But, because language systems or arguments born out of this language do not always engage multiple meanings of a term, other potential interpretations may become momentarily concealed.

The concealing of other interpretations is precisely what has occurred in the construction of popular cultural images of pirates. By definition, pirate refers to one who robs or commits illegal violence at sea or on the shores of the sea, which is in keeping with the images constructed out of historical and literary accounts. This definition has been expounded upon in recent decades to include those persons who rob or commit digital pirating of software, movies, or music, to name a few, in a sea of technological space and time for which no specific boundaries exist. The Latin derivative of pirate, *pirata*, means sea robber. But the Latin derivative also includes roots in the Greek noun *piratis* and also the Greek verb *pirao*. *Pirao* does translate into an attack, to make an attempt or to try, therefore upholding the definition of thief or robber engaged in historical or contemporary discursive practices. However, there is another interpretation which makes problematic how we have, and may continue, to define pirate.

Pirao also means to *get experience*. Historically, pirate has embodied a negative connotation: to rob, to steal, to appropriate, to plunder. But this negative connotation actually negates its own definition in that getting experience can be both a negative and/or a positive encounter. I ask you, what individual living on Earth today does not *get experience* from each moment that is lived? Could not this experience be considered positive in that it reflects an experience of life itself, regardless of whether this moment encompasses feelings of pain and anguish or laughter and joy? What individual does not experience texts, images, technologies, the environments in which we dwell and the constructions that emerge as a result? How do we interact with multiple epistemologies if we do not first experience questions and/or quests for knowledge? How may we engage in ontological endeavors without considering how we gained insight into our being through the experience of living? If we ignored these questions, then how would our being ever be considered Becoming?

Heidegger tells us language is a "'house of being'...because language, as saying, is the mode of Appropriation" (1971, p. 135). Saying, as Heidegger informs, is how appropriation speaks as it shows itself through the process of appropriation. He tells us, "*The moving force in Showing of Saying is Owning*" (1971, p. 127, emphasis in original), not in the sense of owning as possessing for no one "owns" language, but in the sense that through language, we may come to understand more about ourselves as new meanings show themselves and are understood. Thus, owning, as appropriation, is the owning of the *experience* of appropriating new meanings *as we name them*. It is the process itself which Heidegger refers to as being "on the way to language." This way, this appropriation, is the "getting" of the experience of language, and "getting experience" can be interpreted as pirating meaning as we understand it.

Yet for three hundred years pirate as a negative term has been accepted as a cultural norm which has failed to be challenged by virtue of the very language which has constructed its meaning. Let us take Socrates as a brief example. All we know of him is what Plato scribed or, more specifically, our appropriation of Plato's words as we understand them. Likewise, our interpretation of pirate rests solely on how we appropriate the meaning others have conveyed over the centuries. If we accept uncontested these meanings, we perpetuate through silence an ignorance of a possibility that pirate may also be a positive affirmation. No matter if Plato's interpretation of Socrates' words were recorded verbatim, this interpretation has already inculcated our being. And like our understanding of Socrates through Plato, it makes no difference whether Johnson was a man in his own right or a pseudonym for a playwright or Daniel Defoe, for our present-day interpretation of pirate has been largely understood through direct or indirect interpretations of *The General History of Pyrates*. No matter who authored this seminal text, its meaning has already inculcated our being through its influence on fiction, film and other popular cultural texts in which we interact.

In light of this uncontested appropriation centuries in the making, I now ask that consideration be given to the idea that, not only Derrida, but *all humans* are pirates because we all *get experience*, as I stated when I claimed you and I were already a part of the image. I do not wish to offer the verb *pirao* or its offspring *pirate* as an essential form of being, for the experiences we engage are rich with diversity stemming from our own relationships with myriad environments in which we dwell. By exploring the possibility that, by its own definition, we are *all pirates* because we all *get experience*, we may bring to consciousness how we extract meaning from these experiences and how the term pirate evolved to reflect only the negativity historically associated with that term. And while I do not necessarily believe Derrida would claim to be a pirate, I do believe he would explore the conditions for which the cultural construction of piracy has emerged out of its opposition to that of a privateer given his desire to suspend words and meaning into free play. Through this free play, I also believe Derrida would identify the act of labeling one a pirate as nothing more than a reflection of the *pharmakon*, in that the interpretation was meant to poison one's minds *against* these individuals, concealing a potential healing effect as we contest its meaning. In other words, pirates were scapegoats for a society wrenched in violence associated with colonial and imperial control.

TEACHERS AS PIRATES

The final question to consider then is how, exactly, all of this relates to the teacher in my image. As I viewed Disney's interpretations of *Pirates of the Caribbean*, I found myself asking, at what point had Davy Jones been miseducated in such a way that promulgated his corruption, and thus the corruption of others? Whatever signified the point at which Jones became corrupt, many with whom he came into contact also embodied that corruption through choice; a choice always premised with the eerie sound of Jones's guttural voice asking his victim, "Tell me, do you feel death yet?" (*Dead Man's Chest*, 2006). Of course, the choice given was not much of one: die instantly at the hand of Jones's sword or exchange death for one hundred years of service aboard Jones's ship, *The Flying Dutchman*, which equated to a death by prolonged extension. If his victims chose the latter, their physical form soon mutated into a monstrous figure and they literally became "part of the ship" (*Dead Man's Chest*, 2006; *At World's End*, 2007) because they had chosen to become part of a corrupted crew.

The complexity of the plot of these movies mimics the complexity of educational institutions in which teachers dwell; a complexity contingent upon the policies, procedures, and norms of the future and present while historically situated within those of the past. Thus, we may ask the same question of educators that I posed of Davy Jones: At what point may teachers become miseducated in such a way that promulgates an already corrupt interpretation of learning via standards and testing, distracting us from a libratory praxis? Once we educators recognize a particular site or act as possessing the potential for corruption, how may we respond in such a way that promotes continuous consciousness of this potentiality as it constructs while simultaneously being constructed within the catachresis?

I do not wish to mislead the reader into believing I compare the corruption and heartless acts of Davy Jones to that of a teacher. On the contrary, what I hope to accomplish is a demonstration of what can happen to our own souls, and thus the souls of our students. If we choose to ignore potential sites of corruption due to our contractual relationship with the state, our modern-day "Letter of Marque," we may suffer a fate no less violent and grotesque as Jones himself, forever silenced in the abysmal sea of "red tape" and political name-calling and rhetoric. What I seek to explore is how the educational implications embedded within the texts of *Pirates of the Caribbean* speak directly to a time period where past and future collide with the present via the same imperial strategies implemented during the Golden Age of Piracy. In this light, many teachers embody, not Jones, but the pirates who fight against him and also Lord Cutler Beckett in the name of hope, freedom, and social justice.

The society of yesterday is very similar to the society of today in relation to imperialism and colonialism of the past with neoliberal interpretations of globalization and neocolonial control of developing nations of the present. The rhetoric associated with the delegitimizing of pirates is similar to rhetoric associated with the delegitimizing of teachers as specific cable news networks such as Fox News work to poison the minds of the public against teachers in order to pave the way for privatization in the future (explored in chapter Four). In my image, the teacher plays a minimal role, having been reduced to a technician whose only task is to take attendance and maintain order in her classroom. She represents the limited role for which teachers are being reduced in a consumer-driven society whose only product of concern appears to be those generated out of test scores. If there is any person who should embody the definition of pirate as *getting experience*, a teacher should be that person. She must experience the reclamation of classroom spaces as cultural and critical pedagogical seascapes for which meaning is constantly contested and explored. Like historical pirates, contemporary teachers are positioned as the proverbial scapegoats of societal ills. Like the pirates of the past, teachers are struggling for the hope and freedom to define the conditions through which knowledge is obtained outside of dominating discourses on testing.

The present and the past are engaged in a complicated conversation, but I fear we may not be listening. Pinar suggests "'Complicated Conversation' is the central concept in contemporary curriculum studies in the United States. It is...the idea that keeps hope alive" (2004, xiii). Complicated conversation, to Pinar, is a curriculum which invites educators to "talk back" to those who seek to limit our roles in our own classrooms. But Pinar also believes complicated conversation can be conducted within the self, where self-reflexivity and thoughtful consideration of the power struggles emerging both *within* and *out of* our actions may be contested.

As Pinar further suggests, "Curriculum as complicated conversation invites students to encounter themselves and the world they inhabit through academic knowledge, popular culture, grounded in their own lived experience" (2004, p. 208). This means constructing conditions in classroom spaces which promote connections to the world in which students live. No doubt these experiences must be pirated from a rigid schedule of teaching prescribed standards and a test curriculum while the captain of the ship, the school, watches intently for even the slightest sign of a mutiny. And yet, these experiences also define piracy as *getting experience*, for each moment we seek to explore modalities of authentic learning for ourselves and our students is a piratical moment, a moment of possibilities. If we do not become cognizant of these possibilities, then what is portrayed as the miseducation of Davy Jones, divulged as we embark together on our voyage towards understanding, may very well become our own.

CHAPTER 2

FROM PAST PIRATES TO POST-PIRACY

READING THE HOOKS AND CRANNIES

Chapter one introduced us to the social construction of pirate and the relative stability of its association with negativity, thievery, and murder, over time. This was in effort to engage Michael Peters' historiographies as "encouraging the greater awareness of the constructedness of disciplinary history and their ability to wrongfoot us" (2011, p. 218). Peters argues now that the major texts within postmodern frameworks have been established, new writings will extend out from these texts, into the peripheries of culture and society where the relationship between power and resistance exists in its most subtle and nuanced forms. The "canon" of pirate history was established centuries ago through *The General History of Pyrates*, with this history re-presented in myriad formations through the work of Cordingly, (1996), Gosse (1988/1932), Konstam (2006), Lewis (2008), Parry (2006), Rediker (1987), and Sanders (2007). This list is by no means all-inclusive and does not represent the plethora of individual pirate histories written about Blackbeard, Captain Kidd, Bartholomew Roberts and a host of others sailing the seas under a pirate's flag during the Golden Age of Piracy. But while these and other authors explored pirate history, none engage a historiography which exposes the wrongdoing within its constructedness, instead perpetuating that wrongdoing through the absence of any trace; namely, that pirate also means to get experience. My writing serves as a corrective to this oversight while also exploring the constructedness for its cultural impact on current interpretations and what we may learn from this process.

Patti Lather argues the question of postmodernism asks, "How do our very efforts to liberate perpetuate the relations of dominance?" (1991, p. 16). This is the question framing this chapter's reading of *Pirates of the Caribbean*, where Sparrow's interpretation of freedom and our consent to this interpretation fails to liberate us from the larger systems we resist. The postmodern question is also located in John Fiske's interpretation of popular culture where the popular is constructed within the relationship it has with these structures of dominance. To Fiske, popular culture "is always in process" (1989, p. 3), where the relationship occurs as a text, image, clothing, language, video, etc. is being read. What postmodernism offers, then, are multiple readings of a text to explore how our acts of resistance inadvertently perpetuate that which we are resisting. Indeed, Weaver and Daspit caution us against the dominating effects one reading of a text may engender, telling us "any reading of popular culture texts should reflect multiple readings that often contradict each other or act independently from each other" (2000, xix). This is precisely why my framework consists of multiple theoretical lenses and particular authors' perspectives in each chapter in an effort to question the cultural construction of piracy, to resist the new branding of piracy as "just another business model" (Mason, 2008, p. 8), and to open the term to the possibilities *pirao* entails.

Interestingly, one of the critiques against postmodernism is that it fails to challenge capitalism (see Atkinson, 2002; Cole & Hill, 1995; Rikowski & McLaren, 2002). I will discuss this critique in relation to postcolonialism and Marxism in chapter three, along with Marx's own interpretation of the East India Company through several editorials written during that time period. At this time, I wish only to suggest that capitalism is itself framed within a larger system of language in which it thrives on the unconscious consent of the individual to perpetuate its power. Atkinson, in particular, explores this critique in relation to arguments posed by Cole, Hill, and Rikowski, where they declare postmodernism to be a "theoretical virus which paralyzes progressive thought, politics and practice" (1997, pp. 187-188). To Cole *et al.*, postmodernism is a "destructive force" promoting "radical right" agendas and politics. This is a common misconception in postmodern readings; one in which Derrida addresses directly. Many scholars writing under the umbrella of postmodern theory engage Derrida's deconstruction as a way to examine the language which perpetuates power. Lather terms this "deconstructive pedagogy," where language usage and its categories is precisely what is being resisted. And Derrida argues deconstruction is not destruction, in his case, of philosophy. Rather, deconstruction is a close reading of language in order to re-position terms and their meanings, exposing underlying assumptions being used to ground particular arguments; a repositioning where meaning is both different and deferred for readers. Atkinson draws on this difference, arguing postmodernism offers "different ways of seeing the limits to their freedom in the real world" (2002, p. 81), that paralysis occurs when these differences are ignored.

Paula Moya, however, suggests the postmodern approach to difference "ironically erases the distinctiveness and relationality of difference itself... [reinscribing]...a kind of universalizing sameness" (2000, p. 68). Moya's argument stems from what she perceives as "methodological constraints," where feminists scholars who wish to engage categories such as race or gender will be labeled as essentialists. Her concerns also include the broader concepts of experience and identity where she argues scholars will be "dismissed as either dangerously reactionary or hopelessly naïve" (p. 68). This, to Moya, is the postmodern predicament which has had a debilitating effect on those who draw directly from their experiences with race or gender to understand these experiences. But Lather addresses these concerns by telling us, "While we cannot help but be engulfed by the categories of our times, self-reflexivity teaches that our discourse is the meaning of our longing" (1991, p. 119). Categories such as race, class, or gender are themselves sites of struggles between power and resistance; the "trick," as Lather suggests, is in learning how to read our own writing against this struggle *as we write*, and then reflect on what our writing teaches us about ourselves; the "trick," as Captain Teague suggests to Jack

Sparrow, his son, in *Pirates of the Caribbean*, is in "learning to live with yourself" (2007, *At World's End*). This resembles the Heideggarian notion of Being "on the way to language" (1971); that who we are becoming is inescapably intertwined with the language we engage to name the experiences that make us who we are.

Moya, however, exposes a limitation in my own work in that by considering the possibility that all people are pirates, the term loses its effectiveness as a category of possibilities and potentially essentializes all experiences. But I do not assume we all experience language in the same way, or that the cultural constructions emerging out of that language will be similar for all people, even if we *are* always already pirates. Postmodernism affords me the space to question the differences experienced as a result of these myriad constructions. We may use Atkinson's concern on the limitations to freedom she employs as an example. Freedom does not read the same across race, class, or gender lines. Nor does it read the same for individuals within these same categories. Yet freedom is the question to be considered when traversing the cultural terrain of piracy, and freedom is the question being addressed in *Pirates of the Caribbean*. My question, then, becomes one of *how* the Pirate films define freedom, and how this definition presents itself within multiple framings. The remainder of this chapter explores this question and how freedom's representation in the Pirate films intertwines with the polity of our cultural space and time. Against a Foucauldian backdrop, we begin with history's engagement of the public spectacle, extend outwards to encompass more subtle forms of power and control through the films' reliance on the binary between good/evil, Sparrow/Jones, and conclude with emerging means of resistance through which power reasserts itself in society.

DEAD MEN TELL NO TALES

"Though the passing of the pirate has taken some of the colour out of the world...it is difficult to deplore his disappearance. For he was not on the whole an attractive individual: and the more we learn about him the less attractive does he become. The picturesque swashbuckler...makes a very good subject for a story, but in actual life he must have been an exceedingly unpleasant character...on the whole a coward and a cutthroat who made away with his victims because dead men tell no tales."

-Phillip Gosse, 1988/1932, p. 298

With the demise of piracy in the eighteenth century, pirates were forced to find new homes in pirate lore and popular culture as the lands they once sought refuge such as Port Royal, Jamaica and Tortuga on the Island of Hispaniola became the sight of ferocious attacks on their Being. As the King's empire grew, so too did the need to transport goods such as tea and spices to and from its colonial possessions, making the Caribbean and Indian Ocean prime locations for pirate aggression. This evolved into an increase in presence of the Royal Navy and other sovereign fleets in order to escort merchant vessels traveling these popular trade routes.

19

Cordingly reports an estimated 2,000 pirates trolling these waters in 1720, which is large given the sparse population of individuals on nearby lands. By 1723, that number had decreased by half with less than two hundred in operation by the year 1726. He attributes this decrease in numbers, not only to heightened naval patrols and visibility, but also to rewards offered for attacking and capturing pirate ships and their crew. All of these efforts worked in conjunction with new legislation granting authority to colonial court systems to adjudicate and then hang those convicted of piracy against the King, replacing a previous mandate of shipping pirates back to England to be tried in the High Admiral's Court. This became an effective device in pirate eradication through its embrace of the public spectacle (Cordingly, 1996).

Foucault asserts "the public execution did not re-establish justice, it re-activated power" (1977, p. 49). Once pirates were sentenced to death by public hanging, the hanging itself became a ceremonial and celebrated event. Now visible for all to see, individuals were no longer detached from these events as they had previously been when the public spectacles occurred exclusively in England. The bodies of pirates were often left hanging near ports or other public spaces to make visible the punishment in hopes of deterring others from engaging in future crimes. Of course, their hope was constructed out of the fear induced by the spectacle; a fear which did little to alter the acts of more established pirates but was effective in converting the environments of Port Royal, Tortuga, and other safe havens into a bounty hunter's paradise. Once power was re-activated in these ports, justice was redefined in terms of what was just for the King.

The re-inscription of power through the spectacle is interesting in that, in the first installment of the Pirate films, *Curse of the Black Pearl*, our introduction to Jack Sparrow is of him paying homage to this spectacle. As he arrives in Port Royal via a sinking vessel large enough to hold but one passenger, Sparrow passes by the skeletal remains of three pirates dangling from ropes. A single bird of prey feasts on what few pieces of festering flesh still clings to bone. An epitaph reads "Pirates ye be warned" (2003). Gosse's usage of the pirate mantra "dead men tell no tales" becomes obsolete as the skeletal remains speak volumes across space and time *through* the absence of any life.

It is this absence of life which Peter Leeson counters, suggesting "dead men tell no tales" relies on the presence of pirate victims to recall their experiences to others. To Leeson, the popular images constructed of tortuous madmen also constructed what he terms the "branding" of the pirates' image so they could capitalize on the reputation constructed out of that image (2009). This image is what prompted a fear of pirates who did not necessarily need to kill at all, for most sailors surrendered upon sight of a pirate ship's flag or colours. Indeed, Angus Konstam claims the infamous Blackbeard never actually killed anyone. His reputation led most to surrender upon sight of his colour flag (2006). I wish not to negate the probability of pirates engaging in multiple formations of torture and cruelty in their own right. As I stated earlier, there are hundreds of texts addressing this violence. At this point, I want only to demonstrate how the public spectacle participated in the demise of the pirate. This participation is evidenced in Maynard's manipulation of Blackbeard's body for the benefit of the public spectacle. Upon striking Blackbeard a deathly blow, Maynard removed Blackbeard's head and displayed it proudly on the bowspirit of his ship. Legend has it Blackbeard's decapitated body circumnavigated the ship three times before descending to the ocean floor. Maynard's act embraced the spectacle in his public statement of the horror to be experienced when pirates were captured; piracy was no longer tolerated by the King.

Another testament to the power re-inscribed by the spectacle is the actual testament of John Phillips, a pirate whose career lasted a meager nine months before his demise. Phillips' testimony against his assailants depended not on his words but on his posthumous appearance in court. His murderers were members of his own crew who decided a mutiny against the severely injured Captain Phillips was their best course of action, thrusting his wounded body overboard to drown. According to Brenda Lewis, "officers of the court had recovered Phillips' body, cut off the head, pickled it to make sure it remained identifiable and entered it as prosecution evidence" (2008, p. 89). It was *through* Phillips' absence of life, demonstrated via the *presence* of his pickled crown, that these pirates were also condemned to death. His crown made a spectacle of those who wish to defy the crown of authority in which pirates are historically depicted to have done. And it is through this absence of life which historically situates the Pirate films while also serving as a reminder of the absence in modern society of the brutal, public statements regarding punishment and torture as experienced at the end of the Golden Age of Piracy.

The demise of the pirate is a classic example of Foucault's *Discipline and Punish*. Once a flagrant form of punishment, the public spectacle evolved into more subtle, nuanced forms of control where the individual embodies the panopticon, constantly surveying the actions of the self and others, as is evidenced in the number of "landlubbers" who no longer offered protection to pirates seeking refuge in Tortuga and other locations. Foucault argues these new mechanisms of power "are not ensured by right but by technique, not by law but by normalization, not by punishment but by control, methods that are employed at all levels and in forms that go beyond the state and its apparatus" (1978, p. 89). What became normalized through the body of society, extending out to encompass what Foucault termed "capillaries," those minute aspects of culture including individual bodies, was the belief that pirate meant only the negative. Cultural keepsakes such as the *General History of Pyrates* re-inscribed this belief until the pirates association with negativity was no longer questioned. As the distance between the public spectacles occurring at the end of the Golden Age of Piracy and modern-day forms of control widened, a sort of romanticizing of the pirate began to evolve. Cordingly's text chronicles this evolution and credits authors such as Stevenson with the popularized, contemporary image of pirates as we view them today. And it is through these cultural constructions that the deceased pirates of the Golden Age have been able to tell their tales, never once objecting to the embellishments granted through cultural shifts in space and time: embellishments such as treasure maps and dead men's chests, talking parrots and black schooners, most of which may be attributed to Stevenson's *Treasure Island.*

Gosse suggests "it is likely the disappearance [of pirates] is permanent...yet it is possible" (1988/1932, p. 298). This statement adheres to a privileging of speech. What Gosse failed to recognize, however, was how historical pirates continued their speech through multiple writings, fictional tales, and visual images constructed by others well into the present. The initial scene where Sparrow pays his respects to this speech appears to be a direct rebuttal to Gosse in that pirates have not disappeared at all. Rather, they have been dormant, lying just beneath the fluctuating tides of culture and society. Indeed, the first decade of the twenty-first century has witnessed a resurgence of piracy, not only in popular cultural spaces such as the Pirate films, but also in the Horn of Africa, the Gulf of Aden, the Niger Delta, in the virtual world and cyberspace, as well as an increase in the number of arguments engaging a pirate metaphor.

Reading this resurgence of piracy requires what Said refers to as a "contrapuntal reading" which takes into account how processes of imperialism and resistance work themselves into a "vision of the moment" (1993, p. 67). This vision must then be juxtaposed with the "revisions it later provoked" (p. 67). Pirates operating off of African coastlines will be explored in chapter four, only after present-day revisions of piracy have been detailed. At this time, I wish to address the duality between good/evil and how this comparison is being engaged in the Pirate films to redefine freedom; a freedom that present-day pirates seek to obtain. And to address this duality, we must read Davy Jones.

DAVY JONES: MONSTROUS MUTATION OR ZOMBIE POLITICIAN?

Popular culture as a site of struggle and possibility needs to be understood not only in terms of its productive elements, but also in terms of how its forms articulate processes through which the production, organization, and regulation of consent take place around various social practices at the level of daily life.

-Giroux and Simon, 1989, p. 14

When *Curse of the Black Pearl* debuted in 2003, it had to sever the centuries-old stronghold culture had with the pirate as a negative being. This severing was accomplished via persuasion, which Giroux and Simon suggest is how consent is garnered. After Sparrow enters Port Royal, he finds himself engaged in battle with Will Turner. As Sparrow rids Turner of his sword, Turner, recognizing Sparrow broke the rules of engagement, shouts, "You Cheated!" To which Sparrow responds, "Pirate!" Here, attention is called to the identification of pirate as a thief. *Pirates of the Caribbean* acknowledges the centuries-old interpretation, pays its respects, and then sets its course on reconfiguring the meaning. As Turner finds himself in need of Sparrow's assistance in rescuing his beloved Elizabeth Swann from a crew of cursed pirates, the two set sail in search of the ship *The Black Pearl*. The distinction previously made of pirates as thief soon becomes blurred as Sparrow informs Turner that Turner's father, "Bootstrap" Bill, is "a good man...a good pirate" (2003). Similar statements are made by Elizabeth Swann as she describes Sparrow, a known pirate, as a good man, and later Turner, portrayed as a good man, as a pirate. In the conclusion of *Curse of the Black Pearl*, it is Turner who finally recognizes Sparrow as being a good man, thus legitimizing the statement that pirates are also good people. And if Turner is accepting of this notion, surely the audience will as well, for Turner is depicted as the quintessential good man.

This persuasion, however, does not rest solely on the words spoken by Sparrow, Turner, or Swann; rather, the engagement of modernism's dueling opposition between good/evil is employed. Sparrow and the others are juxtaposed next to the infamous Davy Jones and his crew of the damned. Jones has an interesting evolution in his own right in that it was never determined that Jones was actually a living person. His signature appearance emerged out of comments written by Defoe where he recorded "Heaving the rest into Davy Jones's locker," (as quoted in Curran, 2007, p. 112) in his essay. Curran presents several theories associated with Jones's construction. One popular belief is how many sailors constructed the term "Davy Jones" as a euphemism for the Biblical Devil and Jonah; both names were considered a bad omen to utter while at sea. The Welsh believed Jones's locker was akin to purgatory, where people were sentenced to await the time when a final judgment would be handed down by God. Those of the Caribbean and West Indies believed Jones was not a reflection of Christian Europe but a Creole ghost associated with witchcraft and black magic. These ideas offer Jones as an evil spirit that would "store" his victims on a remote island and feed on them at leisure while wreaking havoc on ships unfortunate enough to sail adjacent seas. Curran's other theories do present Jones as an actual person; from a not-so-famous pirate sailing the Caribbean in the 1600's to a pub owner in Cornwall, England who press-ganged drunken patrons onto ships in need of a crew. What is explicit in all of the theories posited by Curran, albeit in various cultural contexts, is that Davy Jones is synonymous with destruction, Jones's locker is synonymous with death, and that our negotiations with the terms constructing Davy Jones have been a negotiation through silent acceptance of these ideas. To my knowledge, there has not been one representation of Davy Jones and his locker as meaning anything other than some form of destruction.

Pirates of the Caribbean certainly does not challenge Jones's relationship with death and destruction; on the contrary, the films usher Jones into the twenty-first century by constructing an image of what Jones looks like. What has been left to the imagination since Defoe's inscription in 1726 is now solidified through Disney's imagineering of his appearance. A horrid, grotesque looking figure, grey in color with octopus-like tentacles protruding from his jaw, crab-like claws in the place of his extremities, this larger-than-life mutant of a man is depicted as the ultimate tyrant of the sea. What make-up and wardrobe fail to accomplish, computer-generated technology succeeds in bringing to life that which imagination could only dream of: a nightmare.

Lawrence Grossberg asserts:

The specificity of *popular* discourses depends upon the powerful affective relations which they establish with their audiences. Struggles over the construction of the popular are, in fact, less economic and ideological than affective. They are fought on the terrain of moods, emotions, passions, and energy." (1989, p. 107, emphasis in original)

Jones's appearance is meant to induce fear in the audience and engages the affective in that we become emotionally attached to the plight of the pirates as a result of that fear. But what are we afraid of? What about these films engages our energies and our passions so readily that we permit ourselves to ignore the fact that Jones is himself portrayed as a pirate, a robber of souls whose treasure is those bodies he condemns to his locker? What is the difference between Jones and his crew and Sparrow and his friends, for are they all not pirates? I contend this difference is the precise point where the films engage modernism's binary of good/evil as the terrain on which our personal struggle with difference is fought.

This difference is evident in *Pirates of the Caribbean's* repeated message that pirates are also good people and that it is not only acceptable, but encouraged, to embody their plight for freedom. To help persuade us of the validity of this claim, *Pirates of the Caribbean* shifts the focus from good/evil to that which the movies imply distinguishes the two: corruption. Sparrow, Turner and "Bootstrap" Bill are all pirates, and all good men. Yet they are nothing like Jones, grotesque in appearance and worse than a pirate in that he is corrupt. This imagery continues to persuade us as the effects of corruption are further demonstrated in the pirates who mutinied against Sparrow when he captained *The Black Pearl*. Now under the command of Captain Barbossa, the pirates become corrupt through the greed experienced upon the appropriation of Aztec gold treasure, rendering them walking skeletons upon moon's light.

The repetitive use of horrific imagery of those deemed worse than evil works to persuade us to attach ourselves to Sparrow and the others because, even though they are pirates, they are still better than Jones, Barbossa, or his cursed crew due to their refraining from some form of corruption. As we consent to this imagery, the affective becomes a willing accomplice. The pirates' struggle for freedom becomes our personal struggle in that we all want to be free, however we choose to define that term.

We must tread lightly here; there is danger lurking in these waters because *how* the Pirate films define freedom is what we ultimately consent to via the persuasive techniques already mentioned, and not merely Sparrow's struggle to attain it. I contend *Pirates of the Caribbean* presents what Giroux defines as a neoliberal interpretation of freedom. He tells us this concept "is largely organized according to the narrow notions of individual self-interest and limited to the freedom from constraints" (2011, p. 9). This narrow interpretation of freedom is precisely the freedom Sparrow seeks in his plight. As we attach ourselves to this plight, we also consent to this narrowness with issues of social justice reduced to side-effects in his quest to be free from all constraints. Giroux argues this passivity towards social responsibility hinges on the simultaneous notion that power is perceived as a "necessary evil" (2011, p. 10) within the framing of a neoliberal freedom. Jones represents that evil, and his corruption is also grounded on the idea of a freedom to engage in one's own choices. So the dichotomy between good/evil becomes the technique in which neoliberal policies reassert themselves in society, freeing us from social constraints while repositioning us further within a narrow view of our own role in that society.

In the Pirate films, Sparrow collaborates with Turner, Swann and others to fight against Jones. But each individual has his or her own goal. Sparrow wants to be free to sail the seas aboard his beloved *Black Pearl*; Turner wants to free his father, "Bootstrap" Bill from the *Flying Dutchman* and the clutches of Davy Jones; Barbossa wants to free Calypso, the Sea Goddess, from human form in which she is imprisoned, but only in hopes she may help free him from the constraints imposed by Beckett; Swann wants to free all pirates from the control of the East India Trading Company, but only so she may live happily-ever-after with Turner. But Maxine Greene argues these acts are "antithetical because they alienate persons from their own landscapes because they impose a fallacious completeness on what is perceived" (1988, p. 22). Greene argues this alienation is promulgated by an acceptance of a particular structure in society where individuals feel hopelessly trapped. Even though the pirates collaborate, their efforts are presented as the means to an end, a freedom from constraints as each individual defines them. And it is this definition of freedom in which the characters appear hopelessly trapped. As a result, the films engage multiple narrative threads involving the constant manipulation of one another, making it difficult at times to follow individual plights. The one consistency is the dichotomy between good/evil, Sparrow/Jones, which potentially serves two purposes. 1.) The dichotomy distracts us from the neoliberal vision of freedom being re-presented to which we may consent. 2.) The dichotomy serves to remind us that even though pirates are now good people, they must refrain from any sort of corruption lest they (we) end up like Jones.

So the question becomes, is Jones a monstrous mutation evolving out of his own personal choices in which he is free to decide? Or is Jones emblematic of Giroux's zombie politician? Giroux argues:

> the correlation between the growing atomization of the individual and the rise of a culture of cruelty [represents] a type of zombie politics in which the living dead engage in forms of rapacious behavior that destroy almost every facet of a substantive democratic polity. (2011, p. 12)

As a result of this atomization, individuals become indifferent to issues of social justice and become numb to the idea that individual freedom is not without its consequences imposed on others. Giroux cites examples such as Limbaugh, Beck, and Palin for the outright indignation they display towards the Other in their public statements. Jones exemplifies this zombie politics in his rapacious behavior on the seas. He destroys-ships, souls, anything unfortunate enough to cross his path. Jones embraces fear both through the affective and through language. Where Palin might yell "reload" (Giroux, 2011) against a Beckian backdrop of the return of Hitler, Jones asks, "Do you fear death? Do you fear that dark abyss? All your deeds laid bare, all your sins punished? I can offer you...an escape" (*Dead Man's Chest*, 2006). His escape, however, is framed in the context of a freedom from being judged for how one chooses to live one's life, promulgating what Adam Smith referred to as individual self-interest as *the* driving force motivating the movements between society and culture, a force he defined as the "invisible hand" (2003/1776) guiding a capitalist economy; an invisible hand which has been replaced by an "invisible hook" in the world of piracy (Leeson, 2009).

At this moment, when we are engaged in an affective rebuttal against evil, the fear becomes, not of Jones, a "necessary evil," but of the possibility that we are already more like Jones than we care to admit; the culture of cruelty in which we live has already inculcated our being. Like Jones, those who choose to join his crew become zombies, the living dead whose appearances transform into monstrous mutations. Not because of a particular choice, but because of the presentations of choice as being either/or, as if no other possibilities existed. We consent to a neoliberal interpretation of freedom supported by the invisible hand which cares not what the Other is doing for it is in one's best interest not to acknowledge such cultural and societal cruelty. To ignore one hand in favor of the other produces an existential crisis where we not only isolate ourselves from others, perpetuating the atomization of the individual which Giroux suggests encourages zombie politics, but also in repressing those elements of the self which need to be fleshed out and understood. In response, we act as Jones did; we lash out against society in violent calls to reload, or worse, we cease caring altogether. In this light, Jones becomes a monstrous mutation *as a result* of his engagement with zombie politics. All those who acquiesce to his power out of fear of the Other become the living dead where individual indifference literally feeds the monster Jones has become; a monster in which capitalism and the promulgation of corporate self-interest (read profit) has also become.

Punk Capitalist or Postmodern Pirate?

My intention in this text is not to paint a bleak portrait of today's culture and society where the complexities of this culture are reduced to some arbitrary dichotomy between Sparrow/Jones. By exposing the dichotomy for which *Pirates of the Caribbean* situates itself, along with a very brief rendering of the history of piracy through the engagement of the public spectacle, and stemming out to include more subtle forms of power and control, we may be better positioned to problematize the binary and its reliance on corruption. The images constructed in the Pirate films are themselves situated with/in a culture where corporate influence and a consumer-driven economy impress upon every facet of life. As neoliberalism gains momentum through globalization, cultural representations (popular and otherwise) and the number of living dead increases in population through the influence corporations now have on political campaigns, legislation, and educational policies; the space to resist this narrowness increasingly becomes the focus of these influences in order to decrease the space itself.

But as Foucault asserts, "where there is power there is resistance, and yet...this resistance is never in a position of exteriority in relation to power" (1978, p. 95). Power and resistance are inescapably bound to one another at multiple sites. Even though the Pirate films define freedom in the narrow sense, we cannot deny Sparrow is resisting the power imposed on him by Jones, whose own power is granted by his immortal state. And yet, this immortality is rendered a useless power without the desire of Sparrow, and also others, to resist. What the Pirate films neglect to consider is how good/evil do not actually oppose each other; rather, they reify the other's position. Sparrow is now "a good man...a good pirate" (*Curse of the Black Pearl*, 2003); but he is *only* a good man so long as Jones is used comparatively. As soon as a pirate emerges in the context of the larger culture, he is immediately stripped of his goodness and becomes once again subjugated as the Other in order for privateers, or, in the case of our cultural space and time, corporate privatization, to legitimize the actions of private industry as it permeates society. Matt Mason's recent argument on *The Pirate's Dilemma* exemplifies the relationship between power and resistance. Mason's thesis is that capitalism *needs* pirates in order to shift the market forward in new directions. He informs:

> Pirates have been the architect of new societies for centuries: they have established new genres of film and music and created new types of media, often operating anonymously and always- initially, at least- outside the law... Pirates create positive social and economic changes, and understanding piracy today is more important than ever. (2008, p. 34)

Mason recognizes pirates to be good people although this acknowledgement hinges on their benefits to a capitalist economy. To support his claims, Mason interviews Richard Meyer (Richard Hell), a former front-man for several punk music bands during the 1970's. Meyer is perhaps most famous for his construction of the image of the punk rocker with spiked hair and ripped jeans. Drawing his inspiration from "rebellious French poets," Meyer constructed his image as a "rejection of having who you are imposed on you by corporations" (in Mason, 2008, p. 11). This example embraces the definition of pirate as getting experience; an experience of resistance to the power structures imposed on one's being. But just because one works outside the law, as Mason suggests all pirates originate, does not exempt them from a system of power manifesting itself within the larger system of language. When I read Mason's example, what Meyer appeared to be doing was attempting to construct a *new* language where he was free to express himself *with* others. There is a consciousness about Meyer's actions that resists a neoliberal interpretation of freedom as evidenced in *Pirates of the Caribbean*. What happened to Meyer, and punk music in general, was that corporations, recognizing this new space, commodified the look Meyer and others constructed that reflected their resistance in punk style and music

(Mason, 2008). As a member of several bands, Meyer utilized the stage to engage in conversation with the new language being constructed. Thirty years after this conversation began, Mason proclaims "punk is dead" (2008, p. 11), having been commodified by the market and branded "alternative" music.

Mason then argues the "independent spirit" of punk spawned a "'do-it-yourself' revolution" (2008, p. 12) where creativity and innovative ideas allowed others to reject authority and carve out niches of their own. But where Mason views this space as propelling the market forward into new spaces, I view this as the commodification of these spaces. The D.I.Y. revolution Mason cites has been sensationalized through outlets such as D.I.Y. networks on cable and satellite channels. Home Depot's slogan of "You can do it, we can help" is matched by Lowe's proclamation of "Let's build something together." Yet, in the interview with Meyer, there is a consciousness of resistance to the very structures of society which branded the image he constructed. Yes, these forms of resistance did shift the market into new directions, but that was not Meyer's intention. His goal was to remain "unclassifiable. Then they [corporations] don't own you" (Meyer, in Mason, 2008, p. 11). So as these new industries shifted, so, too, did Meyer. No longer branding the punk hairstyle he made famous, Meyer shifted his actions and style into poetry, writing, and art, and continues to look for ways to resist power structures (Mason, 2008).

Even piracy is shifting in meaning, where Peter Leeson contends pirates operating during the Golden Age were strictly profit-driven. He engages Smith's invisible hand and re-presents it as an invisible hook with subtle differences such as the consideration that criminal self-interests relied on cooperation amongst pirates as well as those legitimate organizations such as corporations. Where Leeson differs from Mason is that Mason challenges the negative connotation associated with pirates while Leeson embraces that connotation to promulgate his contention that pirates were *only* motivated by money.

Leeson's reliance on "criminal self-interest" stems from Smith's belief that to serve one's own interests, we must serve others as well. "Serving others' interests gets them to cooperate with us, serving our own" (Leeson, 2009, p. 2). Criminals, or "sea dogs," as Leeson calls pirates, were no exception ("Sea dogs" is a peculiar term for Leeson to use because, according to Gabriel Kuhn, the term actually refers to privateers (2010)). Leeson's criminal self-interest views issues of social justice as a means to individual ends without acknowledging the possibility that pirates engaged in piracy to be free from the constraints imposed by merchant seamen and what Leeson depicts as "captain predation" (2009), where legalized sea merchants sometimes tortured crew members. Even though Mason's argument is firmly situated in capitalism and his advocating for the necessity of pirates to propel the economy forward, he does acknowledge modern-day pirates such as Meyer are not motivated by profit but by a desire to be free. Yes, this freedom is a freedom *from* constraints, but it is also a freedom *with* others to explore the new terrains being created.

The dilemma to consider, then, is whether to negate these acts of resistance due to their eventual commodification or whether to embrace the efforts of resisters and then consciously choose to learn from the limitations imposed on them through the commodification process. Mason utilized the term "punk capitalism" to describe individuals such as Meyer and "to describe the new set of market conditions governing society" (2008, p. 8). In this society, pirates become co-chairs, the limitations are "established ideas" and "outdated dogma" (Mason, 2008, p, 13), and the greatest resource is creativity. I reject Mason's contention of punk capitalism on the basis that his approach appears merely to update the dogma he believes has become "old," and it reduces the concept of piracy as a corporate business model which Mason advocates in his writing.

I prefer to engage the term postmodern pirate as a path to challenge the language system in which capitalism is firmly situated. But even postmodernism does not operate beyond its own limitations. Michael Peters informs "different scholars have suggested that once the meanings of the term have been fixed and stabilized, the life will have been drained from it and the debate will be over" (2011, p. 25). Such is the case with pirates, with the cultural consensus of pirate as a negative. But even though the primary texts were established centuries ago, the fascination with pirates has continued to exist through imagination and cultural images and texts offering new perspectives on how one reads the pirate. Once a stable pronunciation of negativity, new interpretations of pirates are emerging in discursive practices that engage Peters' description of "post" as meaning "'the new,' 'the beginning,' or 'a return,' historically speaking" (2011, p. 24). The return of pirate themes has moved beyond the history of piracy and is promulgating a "new" vision where piracy is reduced to a business model through which we may experience life, but it still maintains that pirates function on the outside of the law, perpetuating the myth that pirate is *only* a negative but now has hopes of evolving into positive consumers in a product-driven world.

What we must resist, then, is this "new" brand of piracy through the very language presently attempting to rebrand pirates as "punk capitalist" because this term ignores how pirates' resistance has historically been against a system of imperialism. And we must explore how this resistance is being matched by those with the power to name them pirates as a way to delegitimize that resistance. In so doing, those in power continue to provide legitimacy to privatization which often acts in similar fashion as a pirate. As Brenda Lewis makes clear, "this [the seventeenth and eighteenth centuries] was a cruel world, and pirates, who frequently came from the most desperate sections of society, often regarded piracy as a way out of its toils" (2008, p. 78). Profit may very well have been a motive for entry into piracy, but it was not the only motive. Piracy provided a path away from the culture of cruelty evidenced in that society; a culture of cruelty Giroux identifies as evident in today's society as well.

Lewis's argument on the culture of cruelty of the past is framed within the economy of competition where "access to material advantage" (2008, p. 78) was open to those outside of the "rich, influential, and fortunate" (p. 79). This economy is consistently reapplied throughout pirate texts and reasserts itself continuously in society and in schools as an avenue upon which power and resistance engage each other. Mason's argument is no exception. The pirate's dilemma he discusses is a corporate dilemma in that industries must now decide whether to silence resisters through legal channels or compete with them by commodifying the resistance so that it becomes normalized in culture until it is no longer perceived as resistance. Interestingly, he cites Disney's co-chair, Anne Sweeney, as saying "Pirates compete the same way we do...we understand now that piracy is a business model" (in Mason, 2008, p. 59).

The idea of piracy as a business model is disturbing in that it suggests a commodification of resistance itself. Indeed, both Mason and Leeson's arguments attest to this emerging technique of power, repositioning piracy in a more positive light, that is, as a "necessary evil" for the benefit of the corporation. Mason relies on the pirates "outlaw" status as a distinction between pirates and legitimate private corporations now co-opting its meaning. Leeson relies on his distinction between the invisible hand and the invisible hook. The former being a legitimate economic principle as viewed by those in society who legitimize this ideology though various acts of self-interests and indifference to social responsibility. The latter an illegitimate act due to the lack of papers offering any sort of validation: papers such as business licenses, legal documents, school and corporate partnerships, political action campaigns, and employee and teacher contracts. What Leeson advocates, then, is that it is morally acceptable to engage in cooperation to serve one's own purpose. Leeson's invisible hook becomes Jack Sparrow, legitimized in the eyes of the audience through the embodiment of his plight for freedom. But is it Davy Jones who secures this invisible hook to the historical depiction of pirates as negative and corrupt people intent on destroying anything in their wake.

This is an interesting parallel in the Pirate films because it is Sparrow who has the established relationship with Beckett, not Jones, as evidenced in the branded "P" on their persons marked by the Other. The mark is also reminiscent of a lesson learned by Captain John Avery, heralded as an exceptional outlaw in that he was never killed or captured while pirating. What Avery learned was that pirates operate on land as well as the sea, and it is to this land we must now turn our attention.

PIRATE CAPTAINS, EAST INDIA COMPANIES AND QUESTIONS OF REPRESENTATIONS

LORD CUTLER BECKETT AND THE OCCIDENTAL TOURIST

In chapter two, I explored the dichotomy between Sparrow/Jones and how the pirate films distinguish the two via the corruption Jones experiences. This corruption is utilized to garner consent from the audience for Sparrow's plight for freedom and also how that freedom is being defined in terms of neoliberal ideology. This, I would argue, is a necessary prerequisite to the third installment of the pirate films in its ability to distract us from the ultimate antagonist: Lord Cutler Beckett. While our attention is focused on Sparrow/Jones, we lose sight of the films' message on empire. This chapter renders a brief historiography of the East India Company as it pertains to empire through a postcolonial lens. In particular, Said's Orientalism will be engaged to demonstrate how pirates were framed within the image of the Orient constructed in the West. Captain Avery's representations against an imperial backdrop open the door for a complicating of the symbolism invoked in the final scene of *At World's End*; a symbolism which permits an expansion of the circle first constructed in chapter one. Through this expansion, we are then able to turn our attention to modern-day representations of the pirates of Somalia and how their historiography impresses on educational settings and Curriculum Studies.

Let us begin with Beckett. An impudent character replete with the pomp and ceremony one associates with pageantry, Beckett commandeers the screen with the ruthless intent to eradicate the world of all pirates. Like Jones, Beckett destroys, but this destruction is portrayed as an acceptable norm in society. As a representative of the East India Trading Company, Beckett does not experience the monstrous mutation Jones experiences for two potential reasons. One being that imperial corruption is tolerable since the corruption works for the benefit of empire; the other being that empire itself is superior to corruption in that corruption is portrayed as a human engagement. In other words, it is not empire which experiences corruption, but the individuals constructing that empire.

The second possibility mimics a neoliberal ideology in that individual alone is responsible for her fate in life, negating the possibility that social injustices and imperial forces also impress on that fate. This possibility is pontificated in the climax of *At World's End*. After manipulating Jones, Sparrow, Turner and a host of other pirates, Beckett's predicated outcome of pirate eradication reaches fruition as the final battle ensues. Beckett proclaims as he peers intently at Sparrow and *The Black Pearl* from a distance, "It's nothing personal, Jack. It's just good business"

(*At World's End*, 2007): good business being the annihilation of piracy so that merchant sailors operating on behalf of John Company, the cultural sobriquet assigned to the East India Company, could operate uninhibited by these vagrant criminals.

Yet, unbeknownst to Beckett, Jones has been destroyed, replaced by Turner's newly immortal state at the helm of *The Flying Dutchman*. With Turner now in command of the *Dutchman* and Sparrow controlling *The Black Pearl*, the two maneuver their ships adjacent to Beckett's and open fire. In a dramatic climax, Beckett, now cognizant of this ironic twist of fate, is seen prudently descending the stairs from the bow as the wooden hull is obliterated around him. What remains of his ship, *The Endeavour*, egresses quietly into the ocean while Beckett's body crashes into the sea. The final image of Beckett is his body being shrouded by the symbolic expression of the East India Trading Company's flag. The message is blatantly obvious: the destruction of the East India Trading Company simultaneously becomes the destruction of empire itself.

The demise of the Company in 1874 may well have been the end of empire if imperialism was only a geographic conquest. However, geography is but one element of imperialism. Said suggests that while there is a geographical conquest of land, that conquest may only be fully realized once the colonized begin to frame their realities within a lens constructed by the colonizers; thus, there accompanies geographic exploitation an ideological re-construction within newly colonized spaces (2007).

Said informs:

> Discourse is a regulated system of producing knowledge within certain constraints whereby certain rules have to be observed...to think past it, to go beyond it, not to use it, is virtually impossible because there's no knowledge that isn't codified in this way about that part of the world. (2007, video file)

This codification has constructed an image of the Orient reflecting less the actual cultural and societal practices of individuals dwelling within these geographical spaces, and more in keeping with Western ideals of these cultures and societies. New constructions emerged not only from actual geographical possessions but also how everyday life came to be defined through representations of the arts, literature and language in general, to name but three cultural examples.

Said was most concerned with how the images of the Orient possessed a totalizing effect on all the inhabitants of these lands. This totality is observed in the writings of Defoe and his seminal text on pirate history. Defoe introduces his *General History* with a comparison of pirates operating when "Rome was in her greatest strength" (1999/1972, pp. 26-27). To Defoe, piracy surged due to governmental neglect. Not until early "barbarians" kidnapped a young Julius Caesar did Rome respond to piracy. Defoe compares this negligence to the disregard British Parliament exhibited regarding pirate resurgence in the 1700's which led to their increase and strength in numbers. Defoe speaks of the "Pyrates infesting the *West-Indies*" (1999/1972, p. 31, emphasis in original), infesting being the operative word. Defoe formulates an initial image of pirate as "pest." However, as a result of parliament's negligence, these pests soon multiplied, infesting the waters as swarms of pirates plagued popular trade routes frequented by privateers and merchant sailors to and from the West Indies.

Defoe then works to dispel romantic notions associated with pirates operating during the Golden Age. He accomplishes this task by providing facts about particular pirates' upbringing. It is not my intention to determine how factual Defoe's claims regarding these pirates were. Rather, my focus is on how his statements advance the ideal of pirate as a negative and also how this advancement demonstrates Orientalism. Let us not forget Defoe was not a pirate himself but an English author (or a possible sea merchant in the case of Johnson) who could not help but be influenced by Western language and culture. While Defoe's travels were vast, his foray into pirate history may be likened to an "Occidental tourist," capturing what *he* believed to be the realities of pirates. In so doing, he assisted in the creation of a Western image portraying all pirates in a negative light, as a delegitimized Other to the privateers operating for the specific benefit of the King and the general benefit of empire.

Let us take as an example Defoe's account of the pirate Captain Avery, whom he suggests the play *The Successful Pyrate* was based. It troubled Defoe greatly that Avery was depicted as "one that had raised himself to the dignity of a King, and was likely to be the Founder of a new Monarchy; having...taken immense Riches, and married the *Great Mogul's* Daughter" (1999/1972, p. 49). Here we see the influence a colonized India was having on Britain's mainland. The Great Mogul is a reference to Emperor Aurangzebe of Hindoostan (India). One cannot deduce from Defoe's writing if the emphasis on the *Great Mogul* is a reflection of a literary style practiced during that time period or if Defoe was intentionally emphasizing a class distinction; no matter how great the Mogul was, he was still an Indian, thus implying a hierarchy between English colonizers and a distinct Other, the colonized. Whatever the case may be, Defoe claims:

> All these [representations] were no more than false Rumours, improved by the Credulity of some, and the Humour of others who love to tell strange things; for, while it was said, he [Avery] was aspiring at a Crown, he wanted a Shilling; and at the same Time it was given out he was in Possession of such prodigious Wealth in *Madagascar*, he was starving in *England*" (1999/1972, p. 49).

The credulity was a direct reference to the play *The Successful Pyrate* which portrayed Avery as a good man; a play which caused debate amongst the public regarding whether to arrest Avery or to pardon him "least his growing Greatness might hinder the Trade of Europe to the East Indies" (p. 49). Defoe sets as his task "the true Grounds of so many false Reports" (p. 50) through his rendering of Captain Avery's life including his actions at sea. One such account was Avery's time in Madagascar, where Defoe suggests Avery's status as "Prince" originated. To discredit this status, Defoe reminds readers "that the Natives of *Madagascar* are a kind of Negroes" (p. 58); thus, even if Avery is a Prince to the "natives," this is not similar to the dignity of a "Princehood" afforded by British Monarchy.

Not only does Defoe discredit Avery, he supports the image of the Orient as exotic being. Defoe describes the "natives" of Madagascar as differing "from those of *Guiney* in their Hair, which is long, and their Complexion is not so good a Jet" (p. 59). Defoe reports that Madagascar had many Princes, thus the possibility of Avery being a prince merely refers to him as being one of many. The "natives" were also simple people who possessed no fire-arms; even if they did, the "natives" were unable to "understand their use" (p. 59).

Clara Gallini suggests mass exoticism as a "type of cultural appropriation can be seen as an act of acquisition, even robbery, that reflects the dominance of one of the two partners in the transaction" (1996, p. 215). Defoe's description of the inhabitants of Madagascar, and also Guiney, are written from his privileged position as European. Defoe becomes the spokesman for what constitutes as "good" in terms of color and complexion. And the transaction becomes one-sided as the words used to mark the description of the inhabitants are not negotiated but imposed on their Being.

Gallini writes of a similar boundary in her reading of a glass curio cabinet and its contents of wordly knick-knacks to question the construction of mass exoticism. The glass is the boundary between "us" and "our" world and "them" and the world we construct on their behalf. We peer through the glass and conclude we see everything. In this incompleteness we are able to construct an image as representative of the whole, a mythical image, an exotic one. The representations rarely tell a complete story. This is similar to our engagement with the Pirate films where the image of the pirate is an incomplete portrait of their culture. Yet we convince ourselves, with the help of the affective devices instilled in the images, that the portrait is whole.

Some of the pirates in the films wear exotic garb and are painted with heavy make-up. But the portrait is conflicting. The garb and make-up speak to the image of the Orient in that pirates dwell in far-off lands, deep within the recesses of our imagination and are limited to the nine pirate lords, the leaders of the pirate pack contradicting contemporary images. But the portrait also speaks of a social hierarchy within the pirate world. Pirates such as Mr. Gibbs are introduced to the audience as he wallows in a pig sty, drunk and doused with the mud and swine fecal matter one imagines when describing filth; nothing exotic about that image, only dirty scoundrels plaguing society. Commodore Norrington, having been stripped of his social status upon his fall from grace with Beckett and the East India Trading Company in *Curse of the Black Pearl*, reemerges in *Dead Man's Chest* also shrouded in the filth of a pig sty. The contradictory messages are read simultaneously: Pirates are exotic because that is how they have culturally evolved, but, in reality, they are filthy, horrid criminals who rob. And yet, if Gallini is correct and the cultural appropriation of the Orient may be viewed "as an act of acquisition, even robbery" (p. 215), then who is the real pirate emerging from the past? That whom society deems a pirate such as Captain Avery, or Defoe for re-presenting them in such a way that was deplete of any negotiations between partners but was dominated by Defoe's own perspective?

What is interesting here is Defoe's dependency on the image of the Orient to delegitimize the pirate. His consistent use of the term "native" acts as a boundary between the inhabitants of Madagascar and those of England, promoting a "them" versus "us" mentality. Also underlying Defoe's description of the natives is the fact that Madagascar was a French colony, compared to Guiney, which, although not formally a British colony until well after Defoe's writing, had established trade relationships with the East India Company. Madagascar, then, is viewed as inferior to English mainlanders both in its relationship with the French and its status as colony. And this inferiority is expressed via the longer hair and complexion differences Defoe cites between residents of Madagascar and Guiney. But while those living in Guiney are depicted as "better" than those in Madagascar, they are *only* better when utilized in that comparison. This is similar to Sparrow being "a good man...a good pirate" (*Curse of the Black Pearl*, 2003) when used comparatively to Jones. There is a repetitive distinction in the *General History of Pyrates* which subjugates difference to a place of inferiority to those of English descent. That difference is not a fixed, stable category afforded to one particular group; rather, it is employed to define anyone other than those reflecting the white, male, European image and who also remain indoctrinated to the rules set forth by the King. This difference is precisely how Defoe distinguishes pirates from other European merchant sailors.

A potential problem arises when exploring piracy from the perspective of Orientalism or the broader context of postcolonialism in that many pirates were also of European descent; oftentimes having been trained by the same merchant sailors who then subjugated them as the piratical Other. But, according to Brenda Lewis, most pirates did not identify with a particular country or law (2008). They claimed no land to pledge allegiance; their loyalties were pledged to the floating land they called their ship. And many followed a strict "pirate code" Lewis likens to a model for early interpretations of democracy. This code will be discussed in chapter six. What I wish to point out at this time is that to focus *only* on the geographic exploitation of colonialism and imperialism negates the fact that geography alone does not make a successful conquest unless accompanied by an ideological reconstruction of one's reality. Pirates, who claimed no land but the ship they sailed at any particular moment, were subjected to an Occidental reconstruction of their own image for the benefit of empire.

To Said, the argument which positions Orientalism as but one aspect of colonialism and imperialism does not delve deep enough into the complex relationship constructed out of the embodiment experienced as cultural texts and images accumulate over time, redefining that experience into one which perpetuates the imperial lens for which it has always already been written. This is reiterated in Ashis Nandy's identification of the perpetuation of a colonial system "by inducing the colonized to accept new social norms and cognitive categories" (1983, p. 3). To Nandy, the colonizer/colonized binary is itself a structure meant to demarcate an opposition between those writing empire and those being written by empire when, in reality, both mutually support the other with varying degrees of violence inflicted on their Being. In other words, one cannot exist as a colonizer without the colonized to oppress. Drawing from Fanon's experience in Algeria (1963) and Memmi's complicating of the relationship between the colonizer and the colonized (1965), Nandy reflects on his own experiences growing up in India and concludes that British influence in his country has worked its way into everyday culture so extensively that it is nearly impossible to identify India outside of this reconstruction.

The same may be argued of the distinction between pirate and privateer. The privateer *needed* the pirate in order to substantiate his own place in society. What may have begun as merely a "pesky" pirate problem evolved into a complex relationship between the pirate, the privateer, and the one element which distinguished the two, a Letter of Marque, which could only be granted by the same governmental agency, the King, framing the conditions for imperial and colonial expansion. So when Beckett suggests "it's nothing personal, Jack. It's just good business" (2007, *At World's End*), the implication is that "good" business is only good *if* it benefits empire. People and issues of social justice are deemed invaluable to an empire engaged in meeting the demands of its shareholders (according to Nick Robins, the East India Company is the first corporation on record to engage in the trading of stocks (2006)). In *Pirates of the Caribbean* and the larger culture, piracy *must* be eradicated because it interferes with the East India Trading Company's ability to earn higher profits.

Yet, in the Pirate films, good triumphs over evil. Beckett is destroyed and the pirates have been freed from the constraints imposed by Beckett and the company. This is interesting in that while Beckett's death symbolizes the end of empire in the films, in the larger culture, this death is merely the beginning of a globalized empire. In actuality, piracy posed only a minor problem to the East India Company and was dealt with by the company's own armed forces, with one branch becoming known as the Bombay Marines. The Marines served to protect the interests of the company by providing shipping vessels protection when entering and exiting company ports along the Indian coast. The real threat to empire, then, was not from piracy, but in the potential failure to reconstruct the *land* environment in such a way that permitted the colonized to identify themselves *outside* of the colonizer/colonized relationship.

This threat is precisely why postcolonial and postmodern studies are vital to the field of education as these studies target the language which has perpetuated the oppressions associated with imperialism. As Nina Asher makes clear, "educational systems, curriculum, and teaching are shaped in context-specific ways by legacies of colonialism" (2009, p. 68). Colonialism did not operate in opposition to empire. On the contrary, colonialism opened a path through which empire inserted itself into the culture and society through its influence on the lived experience. The Letter of Marque granted to the East India Company on December 31, 1600 came in the form of a charter to establish a monopoly trade operating between East and West by Queen Elizabeth I. And it is this charter which licensed the "greatest corporation in the world" (Robins, 2006) to engage in exploitation of the people and the land of India and Britain's other colonies; a license which, according to Nicholas Dirks, married empire to *its* significant Other- corruption (2006). Corruption is what permits Beckett to manipulate other characters in the pirate films in his quest to eradicate piracy for eradication works for the benefit of empire. However, corruption has its own history embedded within the destruction of empire, a destruction which simultaneously becomes its birth, with a history which may be explored through a postcolonial lens.

JOHN COMPANY AND THE POST-COLONIAL QUESTION

In 1996, Stuart Hall posed the question "When was the post-colonial?" (p. 242). Hall concentrated his response to this question on the criticism of postcolonial studies within the context of cultural studies, suggesting a shift "from difference to differánce...[as]... precisely what the serialised or staggered transition to the 'post-colonial' is marking" (p. 247). The shift, to Hall, is in the attention garnered to the mark (/) which has historically divided a privileged position in culture and society from its marginalized Other, and is indebted to the questions emerging out of Derrida's deconstruction. To Hall, questions of the mark "obliges us to re-read the binaries as forms of transculturation, or cultural translation" (p. 247), where colonization may also be re-read as part of a "transcultural global process" (p. 247). From this perspective, Hall identifies the post-colonial as a reading which no longer operates under direct colonial rule but which inquires how the lingering empire continues to define itself within the actions and experiences of the colonized. As stated earlier, Said argues empire is both a geographical and ideological encounter. The ideological impressions on culture and society are what postcolonialism seeks to de-center and interrogate.

Because language is itself a device through which empire re-inserts itself in society, to think beyond this insertion is virtually impossible. The embodiment of language and the cultural constructions emerging as a result of this embodiment is what Spivak terms the catachresis. For Spivak, to acknowledge the catachresis as a space where concepts such as "sovereignty, constitutionality, self-determination, nationhood, citizenship, even culturalism" (1993, p. 71) are already imperially coded within language must be deconstructed in effort to understand how language perpetuates this codification (1993). Thus, to Spivak, postcoloniality is a deconstructive pedagogy which "must teach the overdetermined play of cultural value in the inscription of the socius" (p. 75); failure to acknowledge overdeterminations such as nationhood or citizenship are "the substance of contemporary globality" (p. 75).

Spivak's deconstructive pedagogy converges with Lather's use of the term as both postcolonialism and postmodernism complicate the language engaged to substantiate one's place in the world, whether that place is a colonized subject or an object of some fabled master narrative. And what Spivak terms overdeterminations of cultural values is reflected in Nandy's contention that by "underplaying some aspects of their culture and overplaying others... [the colonizers'] built the legitimacy for colonialism" (1983, p. 12). This legitimacy is reflected in the words used to describe the images of the colonized which provide agency for a postcolonial pedagogy.

But the critique of language is not devoid of its own criticisms. McLaren and Farahmandpur's analysis is particularly interesting in its summation of many arguments posited against the "posts" in general, with their attention focused predominantly on postmodernism. McLaren and Farahmandpur argue postmodern theorists have consistently failed "to challenge in any deep or sustained way the engineered misery of neoliberal fiscal regimes and – more importantly- capitalist relations of exploitation" (2002, p. 43). Although McLaren and Farahmandpur acknowledge postmodernism's insight into the "primary status of the colonizer" (p. 43), revealed the "trace marks of the antipodal" (p. 43) within cultural spaces, and "broken the semiotic gridlock of reigning binarisms" (p. 43), the "posts" in general and postmodernism specifically have routinely neglected the effects a capitalist economy poses on the construction of these insights; in so doing, postmodern theorists have inadvertently reaffirmed these systems and their exploitative practices.

According to McLaren and Rikowski, postmodern theorists have also neglected the possibility "that our lives and 'selves' are, after all, very much centered: by *capital*, as social force and social relation" (2002, p. 6, emphasis in original). McLaren and Jaramillo further encourage "critical educators" to "reject the postmodernist and postcolonial disavowal of Marxism, which is part and parcel of the claim that a Eurocentric absolutism underlies all modern critical thought and social discourse" (2007, p. 86). Spivak would most likely view an interpretation of critical as only legitimized through a Marxist frame as a "limit to knowing" in that awareness to these limits is optimized only when multiple perspectives approach the reading of these limitations. Thus, it may be suggested that just as postmodern and postcolonial theorizing within Curriculum Studies has failed to identify the effects a capitalist economy imposes on the self, there appears equally to be a limitation within Marxist theorizing of attention to the language through which class consciousness, capitalist economies, and imperialism manifests themselves in cultural and societal practices and norms.

Marx's early writings posit fledgling questions regarding the affects language and imperialism was having on a pre-colonial India, and Marx personally scribed his concerns regarding the East India Company in his editorials published in the New York Tribune from 1853-1861. These editorials offer great insight into Marx's early writings as he grappled with questions of use-value, production, the accumulation of growth in capitalist economies as well as Britain's effects on India's economy. Marx has been criticized by stating "Indian society has no history at all, at least no known history. What *we* call its history, is but the history of successive intruders who founded their empires on the passive bases of that unresisting and unchanging society" (2006/1853c, p. 46, emphasis added). I emphasize "we" in the quotation because it is this word which connects Marx's early writings to Said's concept of Orientalism.

Irfan Habib demonstrates Marx's reliance on Hegel's description of Hindoos as a starting point to understanding Indian culture, which Habib also suggests Marx substantiated through other references and did not rely on the totality of "Hegelian generalizations" (2006, xxii) to formulate his construction of that culture. But the critique is that Marx erased the possibility of any history occurring in India prior to its colonization. However, when "we" is highlighted, there exists the *possibility* Marx is not erasing, but recognizing, that his conception of a pre-colonial India is itself a Western interpretation constructed out of the images produced by Hegel and others which Marx drew upon to construct *his* interpretation. This possible acknowledgement by Marx differs from Defoe in that Defoe fails to acknowledge his role in the construction of the pirate. Kuhn notes, Golden-Age pirates are "a people with no recorded history" (2010, p. 118) outside of what others have been able to create, largely dependent on Defoe's account. Yet Defoe's work is not questioned in similar fashion as Marx, but a taken-for-granted norm that his construction *is* the history of pirates, in large part, I believe, because Defoe's description does not challenge empire but substantiates its place in society.

What is of further interest is how much India and the East India Company served as a backdrop for Marx's later writings. As he continued to explore what he termed the Asiatic Mode of Production, Marx struggled with questions addressing the devastating role Britain's presence imposed on the people and land of India; a presence which was producing more dependency on Britain as the latter worked diligently to increase control of taxes imposed on land owners in India. Technological advances were but one arena where Britain was able to increase dependency, with Marx reporting, "It was the British intruder who broke up the Indian hand-loom and destroyed the spinning-wheel" (2006/1853a, p. 14). This intrusion created conditions for an influx of imports from Britain to India and resulted in a decline of population in rural Indian towns. The East India Company capitalized on these conditions, creating a tax-base on property and land revenues, which, to Marx, became India's main export to Britain; as Marx suggests, "The East India Company excluded the common people from the commerce with India, at the same time that the House of Commons excluded them from Parliamentary representation" (2006/1853b, p. 21). Without representation and no voice outside of their own traditions of a social-class system based on property ownership, which Marx was also exploring, Marx surmised Britain had finally "broken down the entire framework of Indian society" (2006/1853a, p. 12).

Again, what is reflected in Marx's writing is an acknowledgement that external forces were redefining what it meant to be Indian at that time. And through British intrusion, a corrupt empire was able to exploit the people and the land for the benefit of the East India Company's shareholders, namely, British aristocracy. But while Marx's attention was afforded to the effects of Britain on a colonized India and a social hierarchy already existing in pre-colonial India, British Parliament, in particular Edmund Burke, had focused their attention on the effects a corrupt India was having on Britain's mainland. As Nicholas Dirks points out:

Empire was always a scandal for those who were colonized. It is less well known that empire began as a scandal even for those who were colonizers. Imperial expansion for England began either with the explorations of adventurers and often less-than-honorable men (such as pirates) or with the outright expulsion of less-than-desirable subjects (2006, p. 7).

This expulsion was precisely how Britain accomplished its delegitimization of the pirate during the Golden Age. By diverting attention away from the plight of the lower classes where Lewis argues many pirates emerged, individuals within British Parliament were able to paint a portrait of the pirate as criminal. This portrayal is almost identical to what Burke painted in relation to India and the East.

In the infamous trial of Warren Hastings (Governor-General to the East India Company from 1773-1785), Burke recognized "India had been pillaged by a growing succession of increasingly unscrupulous Nabobs" (Dirks, 2006, p. 9). A Nabob is the English term assigned to those who made their fortunes exploiting the East and then returned to England. And this return of the Nabob to the mainland concerned Burke, not because of the exploitations occurring in India and to the people and land as a result of this pillaging, but because Burke believed the "new" money originating out of the East was corrupting England, with some Nabobs spending a portion of their earnings buying seats in Parliament and, even worse, marrying into what Burke refers to as the "old gentry."

What Burke was doing was privileging the "old gentry" at the expense of the "new" money he believed to be corrupt with the intrusion of what he considered to be second-class citizens in Parliament. Indeed, Dirks quotes one British aristocrat, Lord Chatham, as stating:

The riches in Asia have been poured in upon us, and have brought with them not only Asiatic luxury, but, I fear, Asiatic principles of government. Without connections, without any natural interest in the soil, the importers of foreign gold have forced their way into Parliament by such a torrent of private corruption as no hereditary fortune could resist (as quoted in Dirks, 2006, pp. 12-13).

Dirks observes in Chatham's words a difference afforded to the corruption being assigned to "new" money without any recognition that old money was also a corrupt accumulation of growth earned off the backs of the proletariats. I also find compelling a lack of acknowledgement on the part of British colonizers that they, too, had no "natural interests" in the soil of India, which is perhaps why Marx accused Britain of colonizing India to make money out of it.

But while Marx was focusing his energies on the Asiatic Mode of Production, Burke was focusing his attention on Asiatic corruption which he feared had illegitimately worked its way into the "old gentry" of Britain and threatened the "ancient constitution" on which Britain had been established. And, according to Dirks, what Burke accomplished during Hastings' trial was a successful inculcation of the idea that, while Hastings was corrupt, thus threatening to corrupt all of England, he only *became* corrupt through the actions, bribes, and the monetary and land grants offered to the East India Company and its employees through an already corrupt Indian government and people. In other words, it was not the Englishman's fault he was corrupt. Rather, Hastings had been corrupted by the people of India. His choice was not his own, contradicting the pirate trilogy's message (to which I will return in chapter six).

As a result, Burke succeeded in constructing an image of empire as free from corruption itself and had rallied the British elite to fight against corruption's influence in England as a form of patriotism. In so doing, scandal became re-presented, not as empire itself, but as an association with India. "It was attached to Indian customs rather than British activities. Indeed, India became a land of scandal in an entirely new way, with scandal now a feature of generic Indian custom rather than personal English excess" (Dirks, 2006, p. 23). In other words, the people of India became corrupt villains for the crime of being colonized. And the colonizers must now work to save the colonized from themselves.

The Hastings' trial was considered a public spectacle in its nine year tenure. It was also deemed a public failure for Burke with Hastings emerging somewhat as a national hero. But Dirks argues Burke accomplished one of the greatest feats in imperialism, with the trial representing a precise moment in history where the greatest scandal occurred, that being "the erasure of empire from the history of Europe" (2006, p. 29). This moment constructed the *idea* that imperialism was normal; the Western images of a colonized India as corrupt was established, and the mark (/) of distinction between the colonizer and the colonized was legitimized. These acts led Dirks to conclude that empire itself cannot be read *outside* of corruption for they are *one in the same,* with the final, lingering scandal identified in empire's inability to be "consigned to the past tense" (p. 35); a fate reflected in Hall's questioning of the post-colonial and the lingering effects of empire, Said's positioning of Orientalism within Western constructs, Spivak's contention of the catachresis as a space inhibited by the codification of imperialism within a system of language for which there is no escape, and Asher's contention of the colonial legacy embedded within curricular texts. So when *Pirates of the Caribbean* implies that empire died along with the collapse of Beckett and the East India Trading Company, this is a misnomer. In reality, the East India Company has had a lingering effect on cultures and societies with its collapse merely symbolizing a globalized corporate empire's infant beginnings.

CIRCLES, SHIPS AND SYMBOLISM

As the prototype to current transnational corporations, the East India Company acted as the premier text in which contemporary revisions of the globalization movement appear destined to repeat. Not only did the East India Company wreak havoc on India's economy, the oppression of Indian farmers to destroy the land for the benefit of the company caused devastating famines in India. The required and consistent planting of crops such as poppies and indigo depleted the soil of its nutrients, rendering the land a virtual dust bowl. The ecological devastation was perpetuated to keep the British aristocracy clothed in fanciful textiles and the poppies produced opium, a major source of profit from trade to China.

The power resulting from the trade of opium along with the taxation laws imposed on India's residents led to the East India Company's becoming a nation within a nation. Indeed, the East India Company possessed its own armed forces to protect its structures and trade agreements operating in and out of India. These forces conducted actions such as declaring war on China when the country prohibited the use of opium by its citizens. But after two wars, the East India Company reinstated its trade of opium despite China's own desires. The Opium wars exemplify the East India Company's lack of concern towards humanity in India, China, and elsewhere and are summarized in a scene from the film *Mangal Pandey-The Rising*. A soldier, when asked why the company has so much land dedicated to poppies, explains how the company forces Indian farmers to grow poppies at a fixed rate to be shipped overseas to create "an entire country of addicts" (2005, DVD). When China refuses to continue purchasing the drug, Indian soldiers are expected to fight and die for the company in order to return home and continue to be oppressed by that same company. Finally, the soldier concludes, "The circle is complete; we call it the free market" (2005, DVD).

The East India Company's oppression via the desired production and trade of spice, tea, textiles and poppies offer a horrid comparison to the oppression of humanity today through the production of oil. While India may have gained its political independence from Britain, the legacy of imperialism continues to influence India's culture and society, with the continued geographic exploitation having shifted to areas with large oil reserves such as the Niger Delta, coincidentally also where piracy has re-emerged during the last decade.

Also interesting is how the East India Company played a pivotal role in the American Revolution and the events leading up to the Boston Tea Party. The tea cast into the harbor that historic evening was tea produced by the East India Company. Facing potential bankruptcy, the East India Company had petitioned British Parliament for permission to ship directly to the American colonies to lower costs incurred by the company and to name its own distributors within the colonies. By lowering costs, the East India Company hoped to deter the colonies from purchasing black-market tea from its Dutch competitors.

In a letter to British Parliament regarding the tea tax and the monopoly trade on tea offered to the East India Company, John Adams wrote of what he viewed as a ploy "to get the colonies to abandon their argument against taxation without representation" (1773, website) by stating:

> ...I would not advise them to try many more such Experiments. A few more such Experiments will throw the most of the trade of the Colonies, into the Hands of the Dutch, or will erect an independent Empire in America- perhaps both (1773, website).

Adams's prediction of an "independent Empire in America" is startling considering the possibility that the Boston Tea Party was not only an act of resistance to big government in Britain, but may also be read as an act of resistance to big business in the East India Company; a possibility not covered in K-12 textbooks discussing the events of that evening. To explore this possibility would be to question the neoliberal foundation for which current definitions of American culture in relation to consumerism and the rise of the corporation has supplanted itself and taken root in educational settings.

Adams's prediction is also startling given the symbolism involved in the climax of *At World's End*. As stated earlier, Sparrow's *Black Pearl* and Jones's (now Turner's) *Flying Dutchman* flank Beckett and the East India Company's *Endeavour* from both sides. But the historical flag representing the company differs from the one depicted in the films and is shown below juxtaposed next to the American flag, forcing one to re-read the binaries presented in the pirate films;

binaries which lead one anonymous Internet source to conclude that it is the United States which has become the East India Company's lasting imperial *Endeavour* (n.a., 2010, video file). This speculation offers an eerie resemblance to Foucault's contention that power and resistance are inextricably bound to one another.

If the *Endeavour* does represent the United States' imperial desires, then the destruction of the ship in the films symbolizes, not the destruction of empire, but a shift in imperialism to more subtle and nuanced forms shaping our own American culture and society in the U.S. This shift has assistance from the American government with the United States now carrying out its own wars such as that in Iraq for the preservation of twenty-first century addictions to oil, assistance from the World Trade Organization with the oppression of both American and Indian farmers by trans-national corporations such as Monsanto and its devastating introduction of engineered seeds in India in order to secure its "corporate monopoly of the seed supply" (Shiva, 2005, p. 121), and assistance from American-based corporations who out-source jobs to India in order to exploit wage-earners by paying them a fraction of the cost of their labor. Evidenced in these examples is how the free-market has indeed come full-circle, with America and its corporations acting similar to its East Indian prototype, with India continuing to be exploited by empire, and with the face of its oppressor donned in the familiar fabric of the bars on the East India flag with the stars fought for during the American Revolution.

But its adversaries are symbolic of resistance. A black pearl is symbolic of wisdom and integrity as well as spiritual transformation and all that is good in humanity; an interesting paradox given that Sparrow is a pirate, albeit a good one. Thus, Sparrow's plight for freedom is to be viewed as wise and pure. And with Sparrow's neoliberal interpretation of a freedom from the constraints placed on him by others potentially internalized by movie-goers, imperialism can now somewhat predict what kinds of resistance will emerge in the future and is free to hoist its patriotic colors relatively unscathed. The captain of the ship shifts command from Beckett to a now established nation. But unlike its predecessors, American-based corporations are remedied of the burden of paying for its own military by capitalizing on a government-funded military who now rallies support for its imperial endeavors including wars by invoking its own interpretation of patriotism.

Yet, on the other side of the *Endeavour* is perched a more authentic symbol of resistance via the *Flying Dutchman;* not the ship itself, but what the ship potentially symbolizes. Sabine Baring-Gould refers to *Captain Avery* as the Flying Dutchman "who appears in weird and terrible scenes and then vanishes into mist" (1908, p. 375), suggesting it is not the ship, but piracy itself re-inserting itself in one's lived experience; sometimes donned with the mark of Sparrow and a limited interpretation of freedom; sometimes marked with the mutation this limit to knowing propels through the grotesque appearance of Davy Jones; but sometimes marked with a hint of authenticity, of rejection, of resistance, to both a society and/or a system of beliefs which perpetuate these limitations and mutations.

Captain Avery's popularity in cultural and historical accounts result in his plundering of the Great Mogul's ship, where rumors of Avery kidnapping the Great Mogul's daughter emerged but were never substantiated. Avery is reported to have looted approximately one thousand pieces of eight including other valuables that were divided amongst his crew. But Emperor Aurangzeb did not retaliate against pirates. His anger was directed at the East India Company's possessions in India. In response, the East India Company promised to capture Avery. Although this was never accomplished, the event provided a convenient framework for pirate eradication to continue with a delegitimization of the pirate embraced in the eradication process, leaving piracy to linger in the midst of pirate lore and popular cultural spaces. But while *Mangal Panday-The Rising* suggests the circle of imperialism and the free market is complete, *Pirates of the Caribbean* teaches us that the circle was merely expanding, altering its appearance and trying on eerily familiar faces; a circle which you and I have always already been a part.

LESSONS FROM SOMALIA: PIRATES, PARADOXES, AND THE ERASURE OF EDUCATIONAL CORRUPTION

EXPLORING PIRATICAL REVISIONS

Recall Said's contention of how the "vision of the moment" (1993, p. 67) provoked later revisions situated within linguistic, cultural and societal codifications of imperialism and colonialism. The vision constructed out of seventeenth century struggles between power and resistance allows for an exploration into contemporary revisions provoked by the resurgence of piracy off the coast of Somalia. These revisions are demonstrative of Foucault's assertion of how power is re-activating itself in the larger society through Western re-presentations of the pirates of Somalia. As stated earlier, pirates such as Jack Sparrow are only considered "good" when juxtaposed next to a corrupt entity such as Davy Jones. Once that comparison is removed, Sparrow is reduced to a social level equal to Jones, therefore establishing a need to erase corruption from the larger governmental or private corporate institution lest these entities become associated with Jones. This erasure provided a framework for neoliberal interpretations of corruption as advocating only individuals to be corrupt, rendering an institution exempt from the human atrocities of corruption plaguing society.

This chapter explores Western representations of the pirates of Somalia and how these representations substantiate the erasure process. I then juxtapose the erasure of contemporary pirate grievances to teachers inhabiting educational spaces where corruption is also being erased through institutional policies such as Obama's *Race to the Top* initiative. In so doing, not only do the possibilities of *pirao* become evident, but so, too, does the need for an outlaw pedagogy as both a resistance to the delegitimization we, as teachers, are experiencing, as well as a rejection of having corruption erased from the educational institution for which we are a part.

Gazing at a Portrait of Somalia

I say gazing because that is what I am doing: staring at an image of a people the U.S. has already constructed, studying it, reading what it means. I have already discussed the construction of piracy as having always been a Western representation. But how does this construction relate to contemporary representations of the pirates of Somalia? The answer lay in the portrait. Like pirates, what we know about Somalia has been constructed through imperial and colonial codifications embedded within Western languages, painting a portrait reflecting these codifications rather than the realities of Somali people. These portraits have consisted either of a Somalia comprised of second-class citizens living in a third-world country or a Somalia plagued with corruption, anarchy and violence. Jay Bahadur's recent foray into *The Pirates of Somalia* exemplifies the Western perspective through his introductory statement regarding the region. He writes:

> Somalia is like a country out of a twisted fairy tale, an ethereal land given substance only by the stories we are told of it. Everything known by the outside world has been constructed from news reports spilling out of the country over the last twenty years: warlords, famine, Black Hawks, jihadis, and now pirates (2011, p. 5).

Amidst the images of chaos and corruption, Bahadur offers a challenge to the idea of a region immersed in total anarchy, which is interesting considering that anarchy is a link in the chain connecting the pirates of Somalia to their predecessors.

According to Kuhn, reading a text on pirate history without at least one reference to anarchy is nearly impossible. Thus, Kuhn poses the question of whether Golden Age pirates were, in fact, anarchist. He surmises his findings by suggesting "if being anarchist means to live outside the control of the nation-state, or any form of institutionalized authority, then the golden age pirates were surely anarchistic" (2010, pp. 95-96). This definition, however, fails to include Somali pirates in that they may not have actively chosen to live outside of the nation-state. Rather, there is no nation-state to resist since no formal institutions of government exist resulting from its collapse in 1991. And the nation-state does not transcend Somalia's deeper cultural bonds or the institutional authority developed out of one's patrilineage.

However, Kuhn recognizes that while rejecting institutionalized authority, there were successful "attempts at egalitarian community building" (2010, p. 96) while on board a pirate ship. Thus, there existed a need for a pirate code to prevent the anarchy pirates have presumably embodied in order to protect community members from fighting amongst themselves. Likewise, Bahadur argues strict clan associations and rules support egalitarian building both within and between various clans within Somalia and elsewhere in Africa. The clan provides Somalis a sense of belonging. And even when clan distinctions are made, there is a communal connection all clans share through their ancestral relation to a single father, Samaale, as depicted in Islamic teachings (Ali, 2010).

Bahadur's challenge to anarchical representations provides a framework for his readers to understand how the pirates of Somalia evolved. But other Somalis such as Ali Jimale Ahmed, Ayaan Hirsi Ali, and Ali Abdi would concur to a degree their homeland *is* chaotic and anarchic, and they further cite clan associations as one of the paradoxes of Somalia in that these associations are simultaneously Somalia's strength and its weakness. To Ahmed, understanding deeply rooted clan associations within Somalia has constructed two opposing views. One perspective likens clan associations to a "social club where clan -as a concept- transcends the travesties perpetuated in its name" (Ahmed, 1995, xi). From this perspective, education external to clan teachings may provide glimpses into the realities of clanism potentially revealing these travesties. Yet, according to Abdi, the elders in a clan have been the one consistent teacher to the youth of Somalia who now have no structured educational system as it collapsed along with the government (1998).

Ahmed's other perspective views the clan as a "pernicious encounter" which he argues is detrimental to a *new* invention of Somalia in that it perceives the clan as static (1995). Ahmed argues "this thinking ignores the dialectical nature of reality in which the social/political relations which nurture the kin corporate system are continually challenged by new realities" (1995, xii). This is evidenced in competing accounts of life in Somalia by Ali and Aman. Ali offers a passionate account of her pilgrimage out of Somalia, telling us other immigrants "dream of a time in Somalia that never existed: a time of peace, love, and harmony" (2010, xviii). To Ali, her arrival in Holland was met with a reality that not all countries were marred by tyrants controlling the region or "by the dictates of the clan's bloodline" (2010, xvii). The deeply rooted bonds which Ali might suggest enslave people, especially women and young girls, are reiterated in the narrative account of *Aman: the Story of a Somali Woman*. To Barnes and Boddy (the anthropologists whom Aman befriended), what they learned from Aman was that "patrilineal groups are political groups; politics *is* kinship" (1994, p. 297). But Aman's account differs from Ali's in that Aman experienced a great deal of love in her family, and her resistance to patriarchal teachings of the elders in her clan was supported by her own mother's resistance to being controlled by a husband. Even though Ali and Aman express different perspectives regarding their homeland, both accounts speak directly to a system of relations tightly woven around a patrilineage clan system powerful enough to transcend most forms of nationalism. They also support both of Ahmed's perspectives in their acknowledgement of such travesties with the oppressions of women and the unwavering relationship clanism has with Somali culture.

Abdi instructs during what he terms "the military years" (from 1969 to 1990), Siyaad Barre's dictatorial regime focused on constructing a new Somali language both to promote nationalism, which he hoped would build strong enough ties that would eventually undermine clan relationships, and to free the country from the colonial legacies of Italy and Britain (1998). During this time, Abdi reports massive literacy campaigns emerged to promote Barre's nationalism, increasing literacy rates from an alarming 5% prior to the military years to 55% in the mid 1970's. Along with the literacy campaign, the Somali National University expanded its meager offerings to include eleven degree programs ranging from education to engineering.

Unfortunately, according to Abdi, these successes were not enough to combat the growing tribalism dividing regions along clan lines in an environment where government and the economy were steadily weakening. Coupled with the border war between Somalia and Ethiopia, the military regime, and subsequently, the educational system, completely collapsed. But Peter Eichstaedt faults Somalia's "backwards Marxist ideology" (2010) as its political downfall, failing to factor into his summation the socio-cultural relations embedded within a patriarchal clan system. I believe this to be a result of U.S. and other world powers not recognizing, and thus not presenting to the public, the "unofficial" rule of law reflected in the clan system. Eichstaedt is quick to fault Barre's imposing an interpretation of Marxism rather than report what Somalis offer as a reason for the region's political failure. He was interviewing Somali citizens, but was he listening?

Eichstaedt's conclusion supports not only the Western image of Somalia, but capitalism's assault on anything remotely resembling Marxism or Socialism. I am not suggesting Barre's rule was free of its own brand of corruption. Aman, in particular, cites the military years as her reason for migrating to Tanzania. But to ignore other reasons cited specifically by Somalis perpetuates an image which works for the benefit of the U.S. while further silencing Somali voices. Somalia is geographically situated across from the Arabian Peninsula where a majority of the world's energy resources are housed. According to Noam Chomsky, U.S. supports Ethiopia in its border war with Somalia. Ethiopia, a Christian country, has long been an ally of the U.S: "The Bush administration hopes Somalia will be another ally...This alliance-Ethiopia, Djibouti, Somalia- gives the United States a powerful base right in the Horn of Africa, which is right next door to the major energy-producing regions" (2007, pp. 180-181). However, to date, Somalia has demonstrated no interest in forging an alliance with the U.S. And with the resurgence of piracy, Somali pirates have targeted ships navigating the Horn of Africa including the *U.S.S. Maersk Alabama*, holding cargo and crew members for ransom (or taxes or fees, depending on your perspective), which currently range anywhere from five to seven million dollars per ship.

I will discuss reasons for this resurgence momentarily. Suffice it to say at this juncture that the plight of Somali pirates has garnered a small inkling of sympathy from the world's people. So the portrait of Somalia, already a Western representation, has to be repainted in such a way that negates this sympathy; it has to be repainted to account for the pirates, but only insofar that it continues to reflect a Western interpretation of their actions and not a reflection of how Somalia views the pirate. At this point, the questions we must ask, questions which must linger in our thoughts as we continue gazing at the portrait of Somalia, are these: Who is the pirate in this situation? Who the corrupt? Is it those the West has labeled a pirate, corrupt in their embracement of what has historically been depicted as thievery which is its own corrupt interpretation of the term in that it has historically ignored the trace of the verb *pirao*? Or is it Western representations of the pirates and the people of Somalia to delegitimize the efforts of Somalis because they have something the U.S. needs: a geographical stronghold in a resource-rich region of the world?

Interestingly, in an interview with Mohamed, a Somali pirate, conducted by Bahadur, Mohamad inquired what people in the West thought about them. Bahadur responded with the popular cultural image of the pirate wearing an eye-patch. He surmises, "The romantic stereotype of the swashbuckling pirate was so foreign to the Somali's self-image that my many previous attempts to convey it had been met only with bemused glances" (2011, p. 136). In other words, the image of the pirate as a Western representation fell on deaf ears to a people who have failed to relate their inner-world to those representations constructed by their colonizers and the U.S. So how *do* the pirates of Somalia see themselves? There are myriad responses to this question. But some, such as Canadian/Somali rap artist K'Naan, do not see pirates at all. Instead they see a band of brothers acting in the position of a coast guard, protecting Somalia from foreign invaders who have destroyed the livelihoods of many.

THE ECOLOGY OF CONTEMPORARY PIRACY

The original intentions of the pirates of Somalia evolved out of a need to protect the fishing grounds off the coast of Somalia (see Axe, 2009; Bahadur, 2011; Eichstaedt, 2010). To the pirates, the injustice of piracy is not in their actions, but in the international community's (i.e. governments and supporting agencies such as the U.N.) failure to address their concerns. Abdulrashid Muse Mohammad, a pirate being detained in prison, informed an Al Jazeera reporter "we went into this because of need and unemployment after our livelihoods were destroyed" (n. a. 2009, video file). After the collapse of the Somali government in 1991, foreign fishing trawlers from countries such as China, Taiwan, and Korea, began entering waters close to the coastline, engaging in fishing practices that were destroying the reefs. These reefs were a breeding ground for lobsters and one of the few stable sources of income for Somalis.

Bahadur surmises:

using steel-pronged drag fishing nets, these foreign trawlers did not bother with nimble explorations of the reefs: they uprooted them, netting the future livelihood of the nearby coastal people along with the day's catch. Through their rapacious destruction of the reefs, foreign drag-fishers wiped out the lobster breeding grounds. Today, according to Boyah [one of the pirates whom Bahadur befriended], there are no more lobsters to be found in the waters off Eyl (2011, p. 16).

Eyl is a community which has become a haven for pirate activity in Somalia and also where Boyah spent much of his life as a lobster diver.

The ecological destruction of the reefs is a common thread running throughout all narratives engaging pirates directly. Eidle, a Somali pirate whom Eichstaedt interviewed, argues he "resorted to piracy...out of frustration and desperation after trying to alert international news organizations to the plight of Somali fishermen. 'Nobody was hearing us,' he says, so 'we decided to attack the ships entering our waters illegally'" (Eidel, in Eichstaedt, 2010, p. 33). Indeed, the first years of attacks were limited to a fifty-nautical-mile radius off the coast of Somalia, substantiating the original intent to protect their fishing grounds from foreign trawlers. And it is this fact which leads K'Naan and others to argue the pirates are their only mode of defense against an international community consistently ignoring their pleas for help. Whereas the rest of the world views them as charging ransoms for hijacked crews or citizens sailing seas in or near Somali waters, the pirates view themselves as levying taxes or charging fees to foreign shipping vessels for trespassing.

To add to Somali frustrations, the 2004 tsunami devastating coastlines along the Indian Ocean and Horn of Africa revealed a decade's worth of illegally dumped hazardous material containing "uranium radioactive waste, lead, cadmium, mercury, industrial, hospital, chemical, leather treatment and other toxic waste" (U.N. Report, as cited in Eichstaedt, 2010, p. 38) after it had washed ashore in leaking, disposable barrels. According to Eichstaedt, "The U.N. report said this dumping and other toxic waste violated international treaties that were supposed to govern the export of hazardous waste...[and] was immoral" (2010, p. 38). This led U.N. consultant, Mahdi Gedi Qayad, to appeal to the international community to cease illegal fishing and toxic dumping in Somali waters and for the U.N. to devise "protection, monitoring and surveillance" (in Eichstaedt, 2010, p. 39) of these waters against abuse.

Not only has this protection failed to be provided, but Eichstaedt argues contracts were negotiated at a time when the country was amidst its civil war. This is corroborated by K'naan in his article published in the Huffington Post. He suggests rebel leader Ali Mahdi, along with General Mohamed Farah Aidid, became co-leaders of Somalia after Barre's ousting. But the alliance quickly fell apart after neither could agree on who would succeed Barre as President. The fall-out led to a country in turmoil, hunger, and thousands with no shelter. K'naan states during this tumultuous period,

> A Swiss firm called Achair Parterns, and an Italian waste company called Progresso, made a deal with Ali Mahdi, that they were to dump containers of waste material in Somali waters. These European companies were said to be paying Warlords about $3 a ton, whereas to properly dispose of waste in Europe costs about $1000 a ton (2009, website, para. 10).

This evidences a sense of privilege the West has afforded itself in a global society where boundaries between first and third worlds abound; third-world inhabitants are not worth the money it would take to procure a proper disposal of materials as they are not viewed as full-participants in a global world. Thus, while Somalia had gained its independence from Italian and British colonization some years ago, they are being subjected to a re-colonization effort through imperial means.

So who is the pirate in this situation? Who the corrupt? Those individuals the West has dubbed the pirates of Somalia? This is impossible given they did not commandeer their first ship until 1992, and the negotiations are reported to have taken place prior to this event. Is it Mahdi? His actions exposed countless Somalis in the Puntland area to contaminated wastes leading to complaints ranging from abdominal bleeding and cancer-like symptoms to skin melting off the body (K'naan, 2009). Could it be Swiss Achair Parterns or the Italian waste company? They certainly took advantage not only of a region in turmoil, but also the marginalization of Somalia as a third-world country.

None of the parties in question had any apparent regard to the innocent lives they endangered through contamination. The rapacious behavior engaged by all parties served to inflate a profit margin for the benefit of shareholders of some corporation at the expense of innocent men, women and children. Yet, because these corporations have "Letters of Marques," licenses granting them authority to conduct transnational business, they appear to have also been granted a proverbial "free pass" to engage in any behavior they deem fit. They have also been afforded a reprisal in the authorized version of pirate resurgence through the absence of any acknowledgement to their role in that resurgence. Outside of K'Naan's report in the Huffington Post, there has been little mention of the role transnational corporations have played. What is even more disconcerting is how, through absentia, the erasure of corruption from corporate entities or institutions has led to blaming the victims of these atrocities for refusing to accept uncontested these acts.

David Axe uses the ecological underpinnings of the resurgence to depict the pirates of Somalia as having a "Robin Hood Complex" in that they are stealing from wealthy nations or transnational corporations to feed and finance their own actions; the original intentions may have been valid, but since piracy has evolved into a multimillion dollar business, Axe considers the origins to be mere propaganda. This is substantiated by Eichstaedt and Bahadur's similar conclusions that pirates are "manufacturing consent" (Herman & Chomsky, 1988) from an international community which has consistently ignored the evidence substantiating pirate grievances. It appears as if the consent of the West is garnered through the portrayal of the pirates as evolving into internationally-organized crime cells which, according to Bahadur, has failed to provide any evidence in support of its claims, leading him to conclude this claim is more fiction than fact. But Bahadur concurs with the contention that piracy has evolved into a multimillion dollar business with "outsiders" such as Afweyne, "a former civil servant from the distant central coastal town of Harardheere" (2011, p. 32), realizing early in the resurgence that piracy had the potential to become a profitable business venture. Not to mention K'Naan's summation that Mahdi set his sights on the Indian Ocean as a potential profit-making arena prior to departing from his stint in Somali government (2009).

Bahadur calls Afweyne a "capitalist at heart," (2011, p. 33). This off-handed comment in relation to the pirate as a businessman lends credence to an underlying issue the West may have towards piracy, and provides a possibility for the need to delegitimize pirate efforts via the mythic connection to Robin Hood. It appears to me that what the international community is most concerned with is the inability to *control* pirate aggressions, thus rendering any stronghold in the region futile. When pirates recognized the profitability involved in the ransom of ships, cargo and crew members, they expanded their region from fifty nautical miles to approximately three hundred, fully encompassing the Gulf of Aden which connects Somalia to Yemen and the Arabian Peninsula.

Yet, how different are the actions of pirates from the actions of trans-national corporations who engage in questionable ethics because they are excused from responding to issues of social justice in favor of responding to shareholders via higher profit margins? The difference lay in the credence given to trans-national corporations by U.S. and other governments via Letters of Marques in the sense their corporate licenses also provide licensure to engage in activities otherwise assigned to outlaws for the benefit, not of the privateers and Kings of the past, but to privately funded corporations now ruling the present.

These actions reek of what Naomi Klein terms "disaster capitalism," where private security firms such as Blackwater are cashing in on the need to protect private fishing vessels and cargo ships traveling through the Horn of Africa. Klein teaches "wars and disaster responses are so fully privatized that they are themselves the new market; there is no need to wait until after the war for the boom- the medium is the message" (2007, p. 16). The message being re-presented in the West is that private ships and cargo vessels must now be protected from piracy, offering the pirates of Somalia as a global scapegoat while simultaneously erasing their initial grievances.

Blackwater is not the only security firm capitalizing on the resurgence of piracy. Others include the Somali-Canadian Coast Guard (SomCan). SomCan was contracted by the Puntland government to issue fishing licenses to proper vessels, with 51% of the profits going to the government (Bahadur, 2011). In addition to licensure, SomCan was responsible for maintaining peace along Somali coastlines by protecting both licensed and local fishing vessels. However, according to Bahadur, SomCan began diverting licensing fees from Puntland's Ministry of Fisheries by offering many licenses directly, rendering it able to keep a majority of the profits for itself. Bahadur further reports SomCan also practiced exclusionary principles with local fisherman, preventing them from obtaining proper licenses, and engaged in selective protection in that only the foreign fishing vessels garnered this protection; hence, the same entities which engaged in the rapacious practices leading up to the resurgence of piracy now had their own version of a "Letter of Marque" granting them permission to continue business as usual.

If private security firms fail to provide protection against piracy, Veronique de Rugy has another solution: privatize the ocean. She tells us:

> In an ideal world, we would leave protection up to the owner of the water in question. But today no one really owns the waters where pirates operate. And if no one owns them, no one protects them. Usually governments exercise an implicit ownership of the waters off their coast, but the absence of credible government in Somalia bars that possibility (2009, website, para 1).

Again, we see the influence the West has on representations of the pirate and Somalia. De Rugy's concern is in the lack of *credible* government, not in how some of the *people* of Somalia have chosen to respond to other acts of oppression from foreign invaders. The pirates of Somalia have no "Letters of Marques." Their legitimacy derives from the consent of other Somalis who view them as coast guards, protecting their waters from illegal fishing and hazardous waste disposals. Yet, this legitimacy is deemed a deligitimate response in a world which has already condemned the whole of Somalia for being a region shrouded in poverty, corruption and anarchy.

To suggest the world considers privatizing the ocean demonstrates how deep neoliberal ideology and globalization efforts have infiltrated myriad cultures in the world. Next, there will be conversations regarding how to privatize the air we breathe; water consumption has already been targeted as a private market. One might consider the solution absurd if it weren't for the seriousness de Rugy speaks in her desire to alleviate tax-payers from the burden nation-states have endured while escorting vessels through these waters. I offer a better solution: don't sail in these waters. But, alas, that solution is improbable in that it is less efficient both in time and fuel needs for vessels which work for the benefit of trans-national corporations and oil conglomerates relying on hefty profit-margins to sustain their own class location in a global society.

THE PIRATES' PARADOX

K'Naan summarizes a potential response to the lack of concern regarding the health and welfare of Somali residents when he tells us, "if getting rid of the pirates only means the continuous rape of our coast by unmonitored Western Vessels, and the producing of a new cancerous generation, we would all fly our pirate flags high" (2009, website, para 12). To K'Naan, piracy is a responsible course of action against foreign fishing invaders destroying the reefs and contaminating Somali people in light of the International community's response, which has been not to address original grievances but to dehumanize the pirate and delegitimize their concerns.

Interestingly, it is Governor Swann in *Curse of the Black Pearl* who provides an avenue through which pirate grievances may have been discussed. But, like Swann, these grievances are being silenced, killed, in their Western re-presentations. In the film, Jack Sparrow is being prepared for the gallows. Commodore Norrington watches intently as he awaits the removal of one more threat against the King when chaos erupts. With Turner's assistance, Sparrow escapes his fate. Our last image of Sparrow is of him swimming off into the sunset towards his beloved *Black Pearl*. On shore, Norrington issues commands to pursue Sparrow when Governor Swann intercedes. Having surveyed the situation, Swann recognizes Norrington's pursuit is futile and convinces him not to engage, suggesting "Perhaps on the rare occasion the right course demands an act of piracy; piracy itself *can* be the right course" (in *Curse of the Black Pearl*, 2003). For Swann, not pursuing Sparrow equates to piracy in that it works against the King's command and is therefore also an act of corruption, but that some occasions warrant engaging in piracy when the intention supersedes the immediate action; an insightful comment to say the least and one that speaks directly to the pirates' paradox.

For historical pirates, the right course of action required a complete rejection of institutional laws which had already condemned them to a life of poverty or oppression from captain predation while on board legitimate merchant vessels. They wanted to be free from the constraints and limitations seventeenth century culture and society had imposed on their being. But the only way to achieve this freedom was *through* a cultural elocution which had already branded them the piratical Other. They had to embrace these limitations in order to be free of them.

Paulo Freire teaches "as long as the oppressed remain unaware of the causes of their condition, they fatalistically 'accept' their exploitation" (1970, p. 64). Historical pirates were aware their conditions of poverty would not be alleviated by pursuing a career on merchant vessels...So they rejected the entire system. Through their rejection, they were able to achieve a freedom with others also in search of similar freedoms. Bartholomew Roberts, considered the greatest pirate that ever lived, sums up pirate experiences when he suggests:

> In an honest service there is thin commons, low wages, and hard labour; in this, plenty and satiety, pleasure and ease, liberty and power; and who would not balance creditor on this side, when all the hazard that is run for it, at worst is only a sour look or two at choking (in Sanders, 2007, p. 248).

Sanders argues in his depiction of Roberts' life that it was the *promise* of freedom which drew historical pirates to reject institutional laws and cultural norms of their time; a promise they felt had escaped their reach while living under the constraints and limitations imposed on them via class hierarchies. Sanders further suggests Roberts understood the desire to achieve this promise was both their greatest strength and their greatest weakness, but he and his crew refused to accept the conditions of exploitation honest service provoked.

In similar fashion are the pirates of Somalia. While they do not completely reject either official institutions of government (for there are none), or unofficial authority embedded within patriarchal clan systems (for piracy remains a man's world), they have resisted the exploitation of their neighbors and kin via the decision to protect their own waters. For the pirates of Somalia, the right course demands the act of piracy. Like their predecessors, there is a *promise* of a freedom beyond destroyed fishing reefs, contaminated waters, and poverty. Yet because these actions are not sanctioned by the West, pirates are publically condemned for their actions.

But their struggle is not limited to Western representations; not all Somalis view pirate plights as noble. Boyah, in particular, informed Bahadur in an interview he was aware piracy was considered "*haram*- religiously forbidden" (in Bahadur, 2011, p. 20). Yet when asked if he would cease participating in piracy, Boyah relayed how his plans depended on the reaction of the international community. In other words, he was waiting on illegal fishing and dumping to cease. To date, he is still waiting.

Bahadur describes Boyah as caught between a moral compass equally pointing towards his desire to protect the sea via piracy and towards the land where his actions are forbidden by Islamic teachings. And Boyah's paradox alludes to another contradiction in relation to the pirates of Somalia. On the one hand, they want freedom from others. On the other hand, they take freedom from others: the freedoms of women and young girls. When Ali outright rejected patriarchal oppressions associated with clanism, she was branded an infidel by fellow Somalis. She struggled with the shame she brought to her family and with her desire to be heard. Likewise, when Aman resisted patriarchal teachings embedded within her culture by falling in love with a white man, a forbidden act, she was labeled a *sharmuuto*, a prostitute, which she was not. Then, when she rejected a husband forty years her senior, she was labeled a *nashuusha* which Aman suggests is "very bad...Everything you touch is forbidden to others. Everyone is afraid of you, as though you are a devil" (1994, p. 171). In her culture, Aman was neither married nor divorced, just disgraced. This also brought shame to her family.

Unlike their predecessors Anne Bonny and Mary Read, who donned male clothing to conceal their female identiy and gain acceptance in the male-dominated world of piracy, Ali and Aman rejected the need to falsify their own representations to act, dress, or behave like men, which is how Defoe describes the only two women afforded pirate status. Ali and Aman embraced their female-ness, challenged cultural limitations and catachrestic boundaries through their actions and carved out niches of their own. Ali and Aman's actions teach us the experiences they obtained for themselves were authentic experiences only they could describe. And these experiences were pirated from an already established interpretation of living, whether from existing institutional laws or existing cultural norms. And while Ali and Aman may not have actively assumed the label of pirate, their actions reflect the trace of the verb *pirao* as getting experience. What we learn from these women is there is more than one group of pirates from Somalia, for Ali and Aman embody the trace. As a result, piracy should no longer be viewed as strictly a male phenomenon.

UNDER THE BLACK FLAG OR UNDER ERASURE

Ali and Aman's actions, along with Richard Meyer from chapter two and a host of others consciously sailing under the black flag, demonstrate how historical interpretations of pirate as only a negative is now obsolete; *pirao* as "getting experience" embodies both negative and positive aspects of the lived experience. This holds great potential for educators whose own role in culture and society is being delegitimized in the public sphere from political pundits intent on portraying us as failures: failing kids through failing test scores in a failing school or, at a minimum, one in need of improvement. The descriptions are endless. What we teachers must do is learn to embrace the pirate already within us as an act of awareness working to thwart the delegitimization process.

This embracement is not beyond its own struggles and contradictions. On the one hand, we love our students, which is what many teachers cite as their reason for entering the educational profession. And many of us despise what the institution of education and the testing culture has reduced knowledge and learning to: that which is going to be on the test. We know there is more to life than constructed choices between a, b, c, or d. We thrive on the teachable moments where children seize that moment, pirating a meaning and understanding unique only to them. And yet, because the testing culture coincides with a culture of fear, we perpetuate the reduction of knowledge in K-12 settings by demanding our students learn content in isolation from their own experiences because the content will be tested while the experience in which the content is comprehended will not. I will elaborate on this point in chapter six. At this time, what I wish to highlight is that many of us are unaware we are abandoning the needs of our students. Thus, we behave as Freire suggests- through our lack of consciousness, we are fatalistically "accepting" the conditions through which indifference towards individual student struggles replaces the love we once embodied. And through the indifference we must now demonstrate to secure and sustain our position as teacher, we *become* the instrument through which our erasure occurs.

Furthermore, because piracy has been its own negative construction, we may hesitate to embrace its trace which has historically been ignored. Not many teachers want to be perceived as rejecting the laws or cultural norms of education, either explicit or implied. But neither do many teachers wish to be imprisoned in the laws and norms perpetuating the oppression and recolonization of both them and their students through imperial codifications embedded within the testing culture's language. Like the pirates who believed in the *promise* of freedom, educators also believe in the promise an education may afford to students as an avenue through which freedom may be obtained. Yet, because we are trapped within a larger culture and society dictated by dominating discourses of capitalism, competition and consumerism, enslaved by debt- mortgage payments, car payments, utility bills and grocery needs to feed and nurture our own selves and children- we succumb to the pressures and powers the culture of fear and testing have instilled. We write elaborate essential questions on the board for our kindergarten students knowing they cannot yet read the words. The absurdity gets lost in translation. We give practice tests for benchmark tests to prepare students for predictor tests used to identify which students will likely fail the state-administered test in the spring of each year. The absurdity of spending twenty plus days on tests rather than meaningful instruction also appears lost. But we engage in these practices out of fear of being fired.

One may look to the scandal erupting out of testing improprieties conducted in the Atlanta Public School System as an example of the pressure and fear teachers may have experienced. According to a report filed by special investigators to the Governor of Georgia in June, 2011, 44 out of 56 schools were involved in the alteration of student answer sheets on the state-mandated test. A total of 178 people- 38 principals and 140 teachers- have been implicated in the scandal with eight teachers and three principals having been terminated as of December, 2011. Interestingly, the report implies higher levels of administrative authority- i.e. the superintendent and assistant superintendent- were aware of the actions but only cites the two as suffering from a "failure of leadership" (2011, p. 13).

I do not condone the actions of the teachers in question, but I fail to understand how 78.6% of the schools in a single district can be implicated with no terminations of employment having been extended to superintendents and other district-level personnel. Bowers, Wilson and Hyde, lead investigators on the case, tell us "the 2009 erasure analysis suggests that there were far more educators involved in cheating, and other improper conduct, than we were able to establish sufficiently to identify by name in this report" (2011, p. 2). Thus, the scandal is reflected in the number of educators involved, rendering district-level administrators free of any guilt or corruption even though it occurred on a system-wide level. This scandal is demonstrative of FairTest. Org's own assessment that widespread corruption "is an inevitable consequence of the overuse and misuse of high-stakes testing" (2011, website). Thus, the corruption is not only in the actions of teachers and principals, but also in educational policies such as *No Child Left Behind* which created the conditions in which these actions occurred. But that summation failed to reach the report submitted to the Governor. While the report did acknowledge the culture of fear and code of silence shrouding the school system, it could not definitively connect these cultural constructions to district-level administrators, leaving teachers to pay the full price of the scandal while their leaders were merely slapped on the wrist.

These actions mimic the events occurring in seventeenth-century Europe in relation to the East India Company. Recall from chapter three Dirks's conclusion that the greatest scandal to occur was the erasure of corruption from the history of Europe, placing that corruption into the laps of a colonized and corrupt people of India. It was not the destructive policies implemented by the East India Company or the colonization process which represented corruption. Rather, they had been corrupted by the individuals they were ruling in India. What we are witnessing in relation to the testing improprieties not only in Atlanta but also in Baltimore, Washington, D.C. and other locations, is the erasure of corruption from the institution of education by placing it squarely in the laps of teachers whose choices are being framed as (a) cheat on the test and get fired later, or (b) don't cheat on the test and get fired now. These are the same choices Davy Jones offers his victims when he asks them if they would prefer to die instantly or prolong the inevitable. And like Jones's crew who become corrupt through accepting Jones's conditions, if teachers choose the former, they embody the institutional corruption which created the conditions for which the choice had to be made in the first place. In so doing, they propagate their own erasure. But if they choose the latter, they are removed from their position for potentially fabricated reasons in their refusal to comply with the hidden conditions of their contract.

Of course, one could argue teachers have more choices than to cheat or not to cheat. But when corruption is embedded within the larger institution of education and embraced on a system-wide level as it apparently was in Atlanta, this severely limits teacher choices when they are also enslaved in a system of capital, competition and consumerism. I will return to these choices and limitations in chapter six. What is important here is how the hopelessness teachers may feel regarding institutional education is similar to the hopelessness historical pirates may have felt towards class hierarchies or captain predation while serving on board "honest" merchant vessels; a captain predation eerily resembling current practices of principal, district administration or educational policy predation teachers are currently experiencing.

Like the promise of freedom hoped for by pirates and the promise of education we hope both *for* and *with* our students, many people believed in the hope Obama solicited while campaigning for President in 2007-08. Many hoped *No Child Left Behind's* reign of terror on students and teachers through rigid tests and control would be eased or even eliminated. But Obama and Education Secretary Arne Duncan dashed these hopes through their implementation of the *Race to the Top* initiative, which only exacerbates the culture of corruption *No Child Left Behind* normalized in schools. According to the *Race to the Top* initiative, state departments of education must demonstrate an improvement of teacher and principal effectiveness based on individual performances for the former and school performances for the latter. Evaluations of this performance are used to inform decisions such as whether to compensate, promote, retain or remove teachers and principals from current positions (U.S. Dept. of Ed., 2009). Noticeably absent are the effects *Race to the Top* may have on evaluating district or state-level personnel. What is further stated is the need to "link student achievement and student growth...data to the students' teachers and principals" (2009). This link represents a critical moment for teachers and the erasure process.

When the state of Georgia was in the process of applying for the *Race to the Top* grant, it lobbied state legislators to alter salary criteria for teachers and principals, requesting a percentage of that salary be determined by how well students perform on the state-mandated tests given annually. The legislation failed, but no passage was necessary at that time. What happened through the short-lived and highly vocal debate was how the *idea* of tying teacher salaries and student test scores together began its own normalization process. This provided state authorities the grounds they needed for implementation through the "back door." The debate may appear over, as it has been replaced by quiet conversations behind closed doors in meetings held in the State board of education, state-level personnel or legislator offices, but its implementation is very much alive and well in a public where the seed for this implementation has been planted and is growing.

The Georgia Department of Education also had to prove an allegiance to the initiative. This was demonstrated via the termination of several high school faculties ranked lowest in test and graduation performances across the state. The demonstration affected four high schools in my community of Macon, Georgia, where entire faculties were fired but had the option to reapply for their positions. What this act further demonstrated was the expendability of teachers while the policies, procedures, and norms of society remain virtually intact. Because the role of educator can now be filled by a revolving door of new teachers, the ability to question these policies and procedures becomes limited as those who do choose to question these oppressions can now be escorted out the door to be replaced by new, fresh and naive faces.

While *No Child Left Behind* may have created the conditions for corruption, *Race to the Top* effectively erases that corruption from the institution of education and educational policy via the linking of teacher salaries to student test scores. No longer may the public potentially view education as failing. They need only look into the eyes of their child's teacher to surmise it is *she* who has failed. The institution is awarded a free pass, a reprisal to engage in any conduct it deems fit while teachers are reduced to technicians whose only role is to take attendance so the system, at a minimum, may continue to receive the proper federal funds. The teacher gets an escort to the public hanging as the system tightens the noose around her neck.

Like the delegitimization of pirates in seventeenth century which promulgated privateers to a legitimized position in society, teachers are being delegitimized in the public which promulgates the "need" for the privatization of education. This process was highlighted on *The Daily Show with Jon Stewart* on February 28, 2011. In the episode, Stewart singled out poisonous rhetoric relating to teachers made by political pundits on Fox News. Contributor Andrew Napolitano argued because teachers are guaranteed a student body funded by taxpayers, they "have no incentive to do a good job" (on *Daily Show*, 2011, website). Another contributor argued teaching was "a part-time job...they're done at 2:30" (on Daily Show, 2011, website).

The episode aired at a time when Wisconsin union workers, including teachers, were under assault by Governor Scott Walker. But the language aired on Fox News extended far beyond Wisconsin's borders, affecting those across the country completely brainwashed by the propaganda Fox News constructs and sells. Many in the public now view teachers with contempt or blatant anger. They believe, as Jon Stewart satirically suggested on his show, that teachers are destroying the country. With the alignment of teacher salaries to student test scores, these political pundits now have "evidence" of this destruction.

Like the Hastings trial, the direct line drawn between nabobs, who were portrayed as corrupting British Parliament, and a colonized India and its people who corrupted the East India Company, provided a scapegoat for the erasure of corruption from European history and the corporate mentality. So, too, does the line drawn between teacher and test, virtually erasing corruption from the educational institution which constructed the conditions for corruption and scandal through its own corrupt interpretation of knowledge and learning. The ideological cleansing process we are witnessing has assistance from popular cultural messages such as *Pirates of the Caribbean's* distinction between Sparrow/Jones, with corruption marking the distinction between the two, and with corruption identified as those not in possessions of legitimized Letters of Marques.

But the pirate films contradict their own message with the statement made by Governor Swann that piracy may be a right course of action. In a rare moment of epistemological clarity, Disney Imagineers open up the historical interpretation of pirate as only a negative to the possibilities pirate as *pirao* entails. Yet, as soon as they open the door, it is quickly slammed shut, closing off epistemological curiosity through the death of Governor Swann as soon as Beckett and the East India Trading Company recognize "his usefulness has run its course" (in *At World's End*, 2007). Disney reinserts its power into culture and society in its implication that any form of piracy, of curiosity, will result in death of the body, of imagination, when that form operates outside of imperial control. This death may also be an end to innocence or naiveté involved when believing uncritically that corruption is only a human endeavor. This is the educational standard Disney perpetuates in *Pirates of the Caribbean,* and possibly why Disney produces images and content in films, television, radio and attire that sell innocence, so that it may be able to culturally define corruption for us all, and thus be able to potentially predict future forms of resistance to its own empire (see Giroux and Pollock, 2010, for a specific argument relating to Disney and innocence). Disney Imagineers quickly revert back to the dichotomy between good/evil, Sparrow/Jones, with corruption representing the hinge dividing what Disney portrays as two opposing forces.

Derrida, however, teaches us the hinge "marks the impossibility that a sign, the unity of a signifier and a signified, be produced within the plentitude of a present and an absolute presence" (Derrida, 1974, p. 69). In other words, limiting piracy to a single interpretation is an impossibility given the myriad experiences individuals bring to the reading of a text. There is no one "right" way to read these terms, so the powerful and/or privileged reproduce those aspects in culture that will benefit them the most. And what benefits empire and its neoliberal bedfellows is a belief that only *individuals* are corrupt, not empire, not corporations, and certainly not capitalism. *Pirates of the Caribbean* presents Jones as a mutated symbol of corruption. But Sparrow must traverse these boundaries also, rendering him, too, as corrupt even though he still remains a "good man...a good pirate" (*Curse of the Black Pearl*, 2003) in the trilogy. But if power and resistance constantly engage each other in a delicate dance, how is Beckett portrayed in contemporary cultural settings? And where is the teacher positioned in this tango? These questions require a closer examination.

PIRATES OF THE CARIBBEAN AND THE HYPOTHETICAL MASS MAN

A Conjecture

"I reject...the interpretation of our times which does not lay clear the positive meaning hidden under the actual rule of the masses and that which accepts it blissfully, without a shudder of horror"

-José Ortega y Gasset, 1932, p. 21

ON THE REVOLT OF THE MASSES

"It is false to say that history cannot be foretold" (1932, p. 54), José Ortega y Gasset tells us. Citing examples from Hegel and Comte, Gasset describes their foreshadowing of future events in relation to the advancement of the masses during an industrial revolution where technologies were rapidly developing. For Gasset, prophetic texts are what granted others access to future potentialities in the context of the present; contexts leading Hegel and Comte to foresee potential catastrophe looming just over humanity's horizon unless some spiritual influence was not coupled with advancing technologies.

Nietzsche, however, another scholar Gasset draws upon to justify his own foreshadowing of the rise of a hypothetical mass man, viewed Christianity as situated alongside these technological advances, citing this spirituality as the root of nihilism. Nietzsche defined nihilism as the highest moral value collapsing into itself upon realization of the impossibility of its attainment; a collapse into a world without value; a world amassed in nothing. He argued the highest moral value was the desire for divine perfection; an impossible task given that we are neither divine nor perfect. To be human is to be flawed. Yet, because we may set as our goal both the untenable and unattainable, the goal of a perfection we cannot fully understand as humans, we come to view the world through pessimistic frames constructed out of our failures, clearing a path into nihilism where we gaze into a world now wrought with emptiness. We no longer see the beauty of the lived experience for we have shrouded ourselves in clothing stitched with negativity.

Here, as if foreshadowing Robert Frost's venture into the yellow woods, Nietzsche recognizes two paths. One is familiar, comfortable, where the path has been worn by the trampled feet of the masses, passive in nature, and which demands little effort or no scrutiny beyond "what is"; the other path, less traveled, holds great promise and

61

possibility. This path is littered with the leaves of active nihilism, which Nietzsche describes as both a necessary and normal condition, and also a positive affirmation of the self. Active nihilism is "a sign of increased power of the spirit" (1967b, p. 17), with affirmations emerging after an existential battle with the constraints of our existence temporarily subsides. The brief lapse in struggle offers a gift of understanding where desires now translate into a will to power, a drive to become, not perfect, but the best we may humanly be as we sketch these new interpretations in pencil. The pencil is important to Nietzsche, I believe, because it is not dipped in ink made of dogma. With a pencil, previous conceptions may be completely erased as new thoughts penetrate the page, or perhaps merely crossed out as thoughts evolve.

Nietzsche further asserts active nihilism "reaches its maximum of relative strength as a violent force of destruction" (1967b, p. 18). As new ideas evolve, the violent destruction of what we once perceived as perfection, as Truth with a capital T, no longer holds value, freeing us from the constraints perfection holds dear while revealing a series of lower case truths now emerging into view. It is here where Gasset steps onto the road less traveled, and both he and Nietzsche cast a lingering gaze onto the path most traveled by the masses. After a period of quiet intensity, Gasset casts a knowing glance at Nietzsche, who shakes his troubled head before being violently thrust into the pages of time. Gasset, too, feels the anxiety of a world governed by the masses, but bravely follows the path Nietzsche and others have laid before him.

What Nietzsche identified as nihilism, Gasset called the revolt of the masses; a rebellion against the self also wrenched in a violent paradox between past and future possibilities compared to the world now unfolding. The masses, although great in number, have little understanding of how the path they now travel is carved. For the average man and those like him constructing the masses, "his soul has shut up within him" (1932, p. 68). With all of the knowledge and technologies to which he is now privy, he has no understanding of this knowledge, of the violence incurred by others to create the technologies, or in historical efforts constructed while carving the cultural path which works to define one's place. He is hermeneutically closed, unable to interpret a world beyond his tightly controlled perspective, to glimpse sight of the connections between himself and the environment and to others.

While Nietzsche was troubled by a faith in a Christian moral imperative which failed to be explained beyond a shallow "I believe," Gasset was troubled by the masses having procured opinions regarding the world and of life without any reasoning involved in how their opinions came to be. In contemporary contexts, we hear the popular pleas to what "they" said without the slightest recognition to whom or to what "they" represents. Gasset's words regarding the masses are applicable to our times and worth quoting at length. He states:

> The individual finds himself already with a stock of ideas. He decides to content himself with them and consider himself intellectually complete. As he feels the lack of nothing outside himself, he settles down definitely amid his mental furniture. Such is the mechanism of self-obliteration (1932, p. 69).

We find solace in our capacity to think like others. This is why education is crucial to understanding a world governed by the masses. A concern for both Nietzsche and Gasset was how each respective cultural space and time promoted a culture of mediocrity. Through this mediocrity, average existence in our present becomes the goal because the average man rarely challenges the conditions in which he lives. And this goal of mediocrity becomes a reason for celebration. To cite a contemporary example, on May 21, 2001, George W. Bush addressed the graduating class at Yale University. In his commencement speech, Bush spoke of his classmate Dick Brodhead, who by that year had become the dean of the University, and their mutual understanding. "Dick wouldn't read aloud," Bush said, "and I wouldn't snore" (2001, website, para. 8). Learning for its own sake, a boring task acting as a sedative to the future President, was not a value he appeared to ascribe. He compared his course of study in a joking manner to an "academic road less traveled" (para. 9). I imagine Nietzsche, Gasset, *and* Frost tossing in their graves as they heard these words, for I do not believe this nonchalant attitude towards those whose passion for learning, thinking, and understanding the lived experience was their intent, and would hardly be considered a road *less* traveled. Bush continues, "And to the C students I say, you, too, can be President of the United States" (para. 4). This evidences mediocrity as a goal for a President who would make *adequate* yearly progress the bedrock of contemporary public education just one year later through his signing into law the *No Child Left Behind* act.

As a middle school teacher during NCLB's initial implementation, I witnessed the asphyxiation of the joys of learning for its own sake. Teachable moments and thematic units disappeared from classrooms as the hidden curriculum of high-stakes tests became the outspoken agenda for school administrations. Students trickled further into the background as the connection between the teacher and the test scores produced became a noose strapped tightly around our necks. "All students must perform proficiently," my former principal informed us in a grade-level meeting, "Except those who scored so low on last year's test that we cannot do anything about. We need to focus on those who barely failed because that is what matters when making AYP." This was the moment I realized public education was creeping towards a potential catastrophe others had foreshadowed when mediocrity becomes the prescribed goal. NCLB may have originated to address "the soft bigotry of low expectations" (G. W. Bush, in Taubman, 2009, p. 28), but the policy had merely substituted low expectations for the hard bigotry of no expectations. For those who fall short of proficiency, some schools such as the one I was employed will not leave them behind. No, the school excludes these students altogether for failing to meet the demands of adequacy celebrated by the masses. For those students with an ability to outperform adequacy with minimal effort, they are thrust to the back of the line on the road most traveled to be ignored, not challenged; learning to question the world in which we live is not a part of mediocrity's agenda.

If students dare to dream of a life beyond multiple choice, the test curriculum acts as a sedative, numbing their ambitions until pessimism sets in- a prerequisite to nihilism.

For those who dutifully conform, they will assume their rightful place amongst the masses upon graduation. Their diploma is their admission slip, succumbing to the desires of others and touting average opinions as if they are of their own making. But for those who break free of pessimism, whose active nihilism results in a life-long quest towards understanding, a beacon shines through the masses, providing hope for us all. This is "the positive meaning hidden under the actual rule of the masses" (1932, p. 21) of which Gasset speaks, for prowling amongst the masses are noble beings who understand learning to be an endless quest; the will to power is a will to live life to the fullest, physically engaging *pirao* as one goal is met only to be replaced by another, and then another. For Gasset, the noble person does not belong exclusively to the academics nor is she bound to any particular social class. No, the noble person is *anyone* who strives to learn more about the world; what Nietzsche may have described as the armchair philosopher who dares to question why. The noble person may earn C's in school when the C is to be strived for, earned from the blood, sweat, and tears of good study. The noble person differs from the masses in her refusal to accept what "they" said simply because "they" said it.

There is danger here, where the murky waters stirred by the masses ripples around the slightest sign of vulnerability. Nietzsche asserts "in so far as the mass is dominant it bullies the exception, so they lose their faith in themselves and become nihilists" (1967b, p. 19). The threat to the masses from individual ideals must be stopped lest the ideals become contagious. Thus, the delicate dance between the masses and the noble person begins in elementary school, not only in the classroom, but also on the playground, where the kindergarten bully, with support from his friends either through verbal cheers or silent acquiescence, becomes tomorrow's bully in the boardroom. His power comes, not from knowledge per se, although he certainly learns how to manipulate others, nor does he need any military weapons, although he may have these at his disposal, but from the sheer weight of the masses. Gasset tells us "the mass crushes beneath it everything that is different, everything that is excellent, individual, qualified and select" (1932, p. 18). For the noble person who recognizes her ideas to be different, the threat to conform to the road most traveled becomes the site where self-obliteration occurs because the relentless bombardment against the spirit cannot easily be sustained under the weight of the masses. Her defiance may become crushed as she recognizes the pragmatic ease conformity offers.

Although Gasset argues the masses themselves are powerless, he demonstrates how the *representative* of the masses, the one voice arising out the masses only because he has learned to scream the loudest, has amassed great power. He found strength in his ability to manipulate others at an early age, and has taken his lived experience to the lead of the line down that road most traveled. Here lies another of Gasset's concerns: the conditions of mediocrity which society sets as its goal, and which contemporary school culture appears desperate to repeat, serves as breast milk for a baby whose thirst for power and control is insatiable. Gasset likened what he called the mass man to a spoiled child who wants more, needs more, from a world with a finite amount of resources. The mass man believes historical and technical advances are natural occurrences so he finds no value in understanding how these advances evolved; they are expected, not earned.

Because the mass man cannot fathom any perspective as possessing value other than his own, he is unable to engage in intellectual debate regarding the issues of the day. Other perspectives are a threat to his existence and must be destroyed, not engaged in a dialectical exchange of ideas; the mass man's ideas are the only ideas worth exploring. So he assaults individual characters, annihilates them in public spaces, and portrays them as evil beings whose corruption threatens all should we choose to listen. Through his own actions, the mass man becomes arrogant, believing himself to be above societal laws and cultural norms. Indeed, it is he who constructs the need for these laws by operating to normalize that which is considered different but acceptable and ostracizing that which he deems vulgar and unacceptable through his ability to manipulate the masses. The process barely quenches his insatiable thirst.

Here we arrive in the twenty-first century, at popular culture, returning once more to *Pirates of the Caribbean* where the battle between the pirates and the mass man is glorified through the affective, teaching us that evil is something belonging "out there," "beyond ourselves," occurring only to others who strive for a world beyond average. I like Johann Galtung's description of this act in his identification of structural violence, an indirect form of violence in which a particular oppressor is not perceived, but, recognizing human suffering and misery originate *somewhere*, identified social structures which produce tensions existing between humans, sects of societies relating to race, class, gender, religion, etc., regions around the world, and even within each individual as personality traits clash (1996). This structural violence is celebrated in the pirate films, where the dueling dichotomies between good/evil, Sparrow/Jones, reveal themselves to be the structure violently assaulting any desire to concern ourselves with the needs of others or a more socially-just world.

But who is the mass man?

The problem with this question is that it may be interpreted as a reduction of Gasset's concerns regarding the cultural conditions of his time to the speculative pursuit of one individual while ignoring the conditions in which a hypothetical mass man might evolve. After all, any average person is a potential mass man, able to embody the characteristics Gasset affords the conceptual framing of that existence. For all I know, you could be a mass man; for all you know so could I. Yet it is this reduction *Pirates of the Caribbean* has glorified, fixating much of the images and discourse embraced in the films on the Sparrow/Jones dichotomy, leading to a distraction from other characters who speak directly to a more pressing problem; that problem being how multiple mass-man personalities have commandeered the cultural and political stage not only for their own benefit, but also for the benefit of a more sinister personality also evolving out of the masses during the United State's infant beginnings.

This chapter (re)visits a few of the characters in *Pirates of the Caribbean* by exploring how they support Gasset's characterization of the mass man. In so doing, the door is opened for a conjecture: *What if* Gasset's prediction has reached some semblance of truth in contemporary culture and society? *What if* the conditions that concerned Gasset were expounded upon to include not only those setting the stage for the average man to believe in his own power during the early twentieth century in which Gasset wrote, but also the conditions setting the stage for a particular mass-man personality to emerge more vocal and more powerful than his other mass-man contemporaries within a twenty-first century setting? How would that scenario appear to us? What would they reveal about our limitations? Our possibilities?

Here, I engage in my own hypothesizing of who that contemporary version *could* be. I posit the corporation to fill that role, not to pinpoint the identity of one single person in a literal sense, but to open the door to a complicating of the dialogue regarding teachers, students, and the relationships built between the two as we work towards understanding that relationship. It is my hope that *through* this conjecture, we may identify new pathways not yet taken, guiding us through our experiences in a more thoughtful, critical, and inclusive manner while enlarging catachrestic boundaries as new perspectives are identified and explored for their limitations. The limitations of today become the possibilities of tomorrow, producing a recursive pattern repeating again and again as the ebb and flow of life intercedes. It will be your choice as to what you do with my conjecture. As I stated earlier, my intention is merely to open the dialogical door.

I take as my starting point Joel Baken's interpretation of the corporation as "the large Anglo-American publically traded business" (2004, p. 3), with its history and the situating of the U.S. as the East India Company's lasting imperial *Endeavour* established back in chapter three. Baken makes clear he is not referring to individual corporations or to small businesses, but to an institution personified by the United States Supreme Court in 1886. It is the personification from which I draw in regards to the hypothetical mass man; a personification whose influence in, with, and over society has extended far beyond its cellular make-up of individual and collective beings.

THE CHARACTERIZATION OF STRUCTURAL VIOLENCE

Let us begin with the Kraken. At first glimpse, one may assign the mythical sea monster only a minor role in the pirate trilogy. Yet upon closer examination, it becomes evident the Kraken also serves as a powerful symbol of imperialism. Galtung argues the "shape" of empire is like a center force, with the peripheries extending out from that force. The Kraken's shape as a larger-than-life cephalopod, with a center orifice surrounded by razor-sharp teeth through which it feeds, and with tentacles protruding from the center aligned with suction cups to grasp hold of its prey, is supported by the weight of the water which crushes beneath its depths those organisms unable to withstand the pressure. The organisms implode; a similar observation made by Gasset in relation to the revolt of the masses, and also Nietzsche in relation to nihilism.

Galtung argues:

> Some in the Periphery will be blind to exploitation and brutality and see benefits only. And those who benefit most will start behaving like the center, acquiring Center tastes and idioms of all kind, looking like the members of the club they want to join (2009, p. 13).

This desire is evidenced by the metamorphosis of Davy Jones's crew upon choosing to join its ranks, and whose captain becomes the center of their world in between life and death. Our hypothetical mass man capitalizes on the desire by reminding the masses that his goals are their own via the manipulation of images, the portrayal of news events, public relations, and popular culture; their inner world is reinforced by the similarities identified external to the self. Galtung likens the shape to a tetrapus with four tentacles. The center is re-presented as empire with the tentacles functioning as military, political, economic, and cultural might. While each tentacle may produce massive amounts of destruction in its own right, Galtung asserts when the totality of the tetrapus is at its most cohesive, the effects may render complete annihilation of its subjects through pragmatic and existential assaults. The subject emerges from the assault thinking and behaving like her neighbor.

"The four powers feed into each other for center benefit," Galtung states, "Military power is used to conquer land, resources, producers-consumers, to command submission and to impose culture" (2009, p. 13). The Kraken may be read as the military strength of Davy Jones, intervening only when summoned by its master. The threat of its existence is often enough to deter aggressions against Jones who thrives on the culture of fear imposed on the Other while simultaneously producing a thin veil of security for his crew who believe the Kraken to be indestructible. But Galtung also argues that materials such as land, resources, etc., if not conquered by military might, may be purchased through economic power, with political power overseeing the transaction.

There *is* an economic exchange in the pirate trilogy, with a currency far more valuable than a hefty collection of gold. That commodity is the heart of Davy Jones, with an explanation of how his heart found its way into the *Dead Man's Chest* in chapter six. It is revealed in the second film that "he who controls the heart of Davy Jones controls the seas" (2006). So Lord Cutler Beckett engages the economic might of the East India Trading Company and the military might of both the King and the cinematic version of the Bombay Marines through his manipulation of Governor Weatherby Swann, the cultural curricula embedded within the public spectacle of mass hangings in all three pirate films, and the production of the existential struggles demonstrated through Sparrow's, Turner's, Norrington's, and even Jones's individual reasons for also desiring to seize possession of the heart.

Beckett symbolizes one of many cultural masks the corporation, which seeks to control the hearts of the masses through the myriad ways structural violence is thrust upon society, wears to hide that agenda from view. Lord Cutler Beckett merely conceals the corporate, imperialist agenda while simultaneously offering the audience someone specific besides Jones to despise, especially after Beckett obtains possession of that treasured jewel. Certainly Beckett embodies the characteristics of the mass man as identified by Gasset; in order to be believed by the masses, the mask has to fit secure or that which is hidden may be revealed. And Gasset argued the mass-man exists in multiplicity. How Beckett differs from the larger personality is in his ability to remember. Recall Gasset believes the mass man forgets his past. Beckett recalls all too vividly the pain associated with the youthful rejection of his father, as disclosed in the prequel to the pirate films (Crispin, 2011). This memory is what drives his greedy desire for the power he associates with titles and name recognition. But the corporation's personhood status was born into this world by the verdict of Judge Morrison Remick Waite in the case of *Santa Clara County vs. Southern Pacific Railway*. Waite believed the fourteenth amendment was constructed to protect not only the most humble of society, but also the most powerful (Lugosi, 2006), with the most humble being newly-freed slaves and the most powerful being the corporate persons Waite's ruling birthed into legal life. And the courts have since protected the rights of that mass man dutifully. The corporation's birth was someone else's interpretation, not its own. Understanding potential reasons why this birth occurred is of no value; the corporation only concerns itself with the fact that it is now alive.

Whereas Beckett easily conjures up memories of yesterday, the corporation is excused from historical and technological understanding as these are usually determined to be human endeavors. Because struggles towards understanding are not its own, the corporation expects these advances to evolve naturally, benefitting future profits in the process. Bakon is careful to include those corporations such as Pfizer whose actions have influenced its community in positive and profound ways. But he also argues because U.S. law binds corporations to the pursuit of profit on behalf of shareholders, it cannot fully embrace a human interpretation of social responsibility if that response diminishes financial returns for those same shareholders. Pfizer can only work so far before its actions impinge on the increase of dividends. As a result, Bakon claims the corporation remains "a legally designated 'person' designed to valorize self-interest and invalidate moral concern" (p. 28).

Bakon further asserts most humans "would find its 'personality' abhorrent, even psychopathic" (2004, p. 28) because of its attention to profits over the people dwelling in its community. Yet we accept this psychopath because it creates jobs, to borrow from contemporary arguments evolving out of the Republican primaries in 2012. I find this interesting for two reasons. The first relates to school settings. People entering schools in a post 9/11 world are carefully questioned as to whether they have legitimate business in these establishments and are rarely permitted to roam the building freely even after their business is determined to be valid. The irony is how schools hold the doors wide open for the corporation, the psychopath, to enter through drink machines situated outside of school cafeterias, in the form of corporate sponsorships, the all important contributions corporations make to school sport programs, and through the policies and procedures currently dictating our day, to name but a few examples. Because the law restricts the corporation from focusing on social responsibility if it diminishes profits, the corporation is not obliged to consider whether sugar-loaded drinks are healthy for kids or how policies may harm children, and often sends its army of masses to attack those individuals who raise the question in public.

One such example in relation to children's health is the case of "Cookiegate." In November, 2010, Sarah Palin spoke at a fundraiser in Bucks County, Pennsylvania. At the time, the Pennsylvania state legislature was debating the possibility of limiting the amount of sweets offered to students in schools in hopes of addressing the growing issue of childhood obesity. To "make a point about 'laissaz-faire' government" (Schlesinger, 2010, ABC News Website), Palin brought sugar cookies to serve children at the school she was speaking. Palin was vocalizing her concern that parents are the ones who should decide what their child eats, not the government; a concern which may have led to a complicating of the potential law if Palin would have opened the question for discussion. But by providing sweets, Palin undermined the parental authority she was advocating and inadvertently demonstrated a neoliberal ideal that the freedom to serve cookies is made possible, not via human decisions to refuse items being distributed, but in the corporate decision to market the items to children who may act counter to parental desires. In the process, Palin attacked the Pennsylvania state legislature, reducing the debate to a political slogan of a "nanny-state run amok" (Schlesinger, 2010, ABC News Website), which served her own interests rather than parents.

This example brings me to my second observation. For a political party which holds dogmatically to the mantra of individual freedoms to choose, in itself a potentially noble ideal, what is actually being touted is the freedom of that party to make generalized decisions about what constitutes as legitimate choices by securing the corporate person's freedom to continue producing goods without regard to the negative influence the products may pose on society. This is similar to the East India Company's desire to export opium to China while disregarding China's own desires to the point of enacting war. The rekindled debate on women's healthcare is a prime example. Leaders in the Republican Party such as Rick Santorum wish to override a woman's right to choose what to do with her body in terms of reproduction through their desire to severely limit or strictly define what constitutes as that choice. In response to a portion of the healthcare bill passed by a democratic-controlled congress in 2010, Republicans argued insurance companies should not be mandated to provide coverage for contraceptive use, attempting to "free" insurance companies from the potential limitation on profits while simultaneously reducing the individual woman's freedom to even afford that choice; the limitation is reframed as a choice between engaging in sexual intercourse or not.

The providing of coverage for contraception was likened to corporations having to "foot the bill" for sex, or so said famed Republican mouth-piece Rush Limbaugh.

When Sandra Fluke testified in front of a congressional hearing regarding the importance of contraception in women's health, Limbaugh reacted by reducing her to a slut and demanded that if he had to pay for her to have sex via his own insurance premiums, then he expected her to upload videos of her interludes on YouTube for his viewing (2012, Video File). Remember, the mass man is unable to engage in intellectual debate because he does not perceive any ideas contradicting his own as possessing value. So he attacks the person's character, as was demonstrated in Limbaugh's reaction to Fluke's testimony, reducing her concerns to a punch line of some crude joke in the process.

I liken Limbaugh to the same status as Beckett, as a mask of our hypothetical mass man, concealing the corporation's inability to speak outside of human representatives and cultural representations, yet legitimizing its power via the myriad masks and representations it is able to purchase and wear. The personification of the corporation extends far beyond the reach of independent businesses and overshadows those individuals who wish to use their corporate creed for the social good. This overshadowing was evident in the number of organizations canceling their sponsorship of Limbaugh's radio show after his comments were made. But Limbaugh is a powerful arm of the corporate mass man whose personhood status has surpassed each individual business, so Limbaugh's mask was not stripped completely. He is still on the air selling his version of Orwell's two-minute hate in an hour-long time slot.

Other masks of the mask man include such faces as Santorum and his assault on higher education. Santorum claimed colleges were "indoctrination mills for the liberal elite" (in Bowen, 2012, Website, para. 1). Santorum offered as evidence the "fact" that some colleges in the University System of California lacked any requirements for students to take courses in history; a fact later debunked. On another occasion, Santorum likened Obama, with his desire for all students to attend at least one year of post-secondary education, to a "snob," perhaps attempting to build a connection between the "liberal elite" Santorum believes dominates college faculties and Obama's "liberal" policies. While Santorum later retracted his statement regarding snobbery, no attempt was made to correct his comments regarding the University System of California, leaving those members of the masses who fail to question his claims potentially believing Santorum at face value. For these individuals, the damage has already been done. Santorum has planted the seed of doubt in their minds that obtaining a higher degree is a noble quest, instead leading his supporters to believe the education only serves to brainwash the masses and also future students against capitalism.

Institutions of higher education are threatening to Santorum and other mass men because of the perceived reality that knowledge is power. And because these men, operating in support of the larger personality, have only superficial knowledge of the historical evolution of events, they cannot engage in a dialectical exchange of ideas; their ideas are not their own although the mass men firmly believe they are. Whereas Limbaugh attacks individual character and Palin attacks governmental policy threatening corporate ability to limit human choice, Santorum assaults the institution of higher education because he fails to understand how learning at this level usually involves a deeper understanding of the world in which we live. So the perception becomes the threat. Understanding that perception becomes the site of the attack; knowledge is not power, but *understanding* that knowledge proves to be dangerous to the mass man. Thus, understanding is where power resides.

While these attacks emerge outside of government institutions, another mask worth mentioning briefly comes from inside the organization. That mask is donned by Scott Walker, Governor of Wisconsin. Walker's desire to "divide and conquer" the Wisconsin masses in order to dismantle collective bargaining rights amongst union workers may be likened to Beckett's desire to divide and conquer the pirates via individual betrayals amongst the pirate Lords in order to eradicate piracy. Walker and Beckett sit back and wait for their targets to destroy themselves from within. Like the mass man, rules governing individual actions and behaviors do not pertain to Walker, who avoids the rules by manipulating the law via legal loopholes and economic risk analyses, as is evident in Beckett's manipulation of Governor Swann; the manipulation of Swann provides an avenue through which the manipulation of the law occurs in the films. Loopholes are how the Wisconsin state legislature avoided a requirement that "a quorum be present to vote on fiscal bills" (Sewell, 2011, para. 3). By voting strictly on those elements of a state bill which would severely limit collective bargaining, and by-passing those elements relating strictly to the financial aspects of the Wisconsin budget repair bill, Republicans in the state legislature no longer needed the votes of Democrats who had fled the state in protest of the bill. The quorum was avoided via the manipulation of the law, which worked in contradiction to Walker's claim that the bill was necessary to address Wisconsin's budget shortfalls.

If legal loopholes are not available to the mass man, he may engage in risk analyses for externalities. Bakon utilizes Milton Friedman's definition of externalities as "the effect of a transaction...on a third party who has not consented to or played any role in the carrying out of that transaction" (2004, p. 61). These externalities may be interpreted as individuals such as you and me. They also include individuals dogmatically defending the rights of the corporation; a sad irony when one considers how the corporations being defended place the same external value on the lives of their defendants. To be external is to be expendable. We are all expendable when it comes to profits.

Bakon cites a particularly troubling example of economic externalities in the case of Patricia Anderson. Anderson was driving a 1979 Chevrolet Malibu with her four children in the backseat when the vehicle was struck from behind while idling at a stoplight. The car burst into flames with all five passengers experiencing second and third degree burns. Bakon asserts the reason for the fire was the conscious decision by General Motors to disregard the placement of gas tanks from a regulated seventeen inches beyond the rear of a vehicle to eleven inches in that particular model, among other regulatory oversights, in order to maximize profits. Bakon references a memorandum submitted as evidence in the subsequent trial detailing how the decision to ignore these regulations was based on externalities: out of 500 fatalities estimated to occur annually, times approximately $200,000 paid out towards insurance settlements relating to the fatalities, all divided by an estimated 41,000,000 automobiles on the road, equated to an approximate cost of $2.40 per automobile; a savings of $6.19 per vehicle "if it [General Motors] allowed people to die in fuel-fed fires" (2004, p.63). Bakon's example evidences the degree of expendability human beings are reduced when viewed in relation to the pursuit of profits, and the corporate stronghold over the perspective of the masses as being their own invites these individuals to support this pursuit at potentially their own expense. After all, they may drive automobiles as well.

With the 2012 Republican primaries highlighting the desire for more substantial job growth than what had been reported as of June, 2012, the rally call for the party has been for job creation. No tax increase for corporations, no new regulations on corporate activities, proposed governmental deregulations on established limitations such as the restriction of off-shore drilling, etc. All of these examples are solicited to construct conditions where the corporation will choose to remain or relocate its organization to the United States, thus creating enough jobs to meet its production needs: more jobs, more spending, more supply, more demand, and ultimately more profit. These factors sound great if you are a corporation. But I doubt Patricia Anderson would feel the same way.

The reality is that with our hypothetical mass man controlling much of the cultural images on display, stories such as Anderson's rarely reach other members of the masses, with silence often negotiated in legal settlements. So the faces behind "impartial" statistics often go unnoticed, counter-narratives offering challenges to these statistics often go unheard. Government regulations are re-presented as strictly a limitation on corporate activities rather than *also* a protection of the human beings constructing the society in which both persons dwell.

While corporations are designed to work for profit, democracy is designed to work for people, which does not imply this always occurs regardless of the political party residing in the White House. When the *balance* of power is skewed in one particular direction, people suffer. Right now, we are in the midst of disequilibrium, with the tetrapus's tentacles operating cohesively on behalf of its imperial center and in opposition to more democratic principles which confines the mass man and hinders his ability to quench his thirst. The demise of Governor Swann in *Pirates of the Caribbean* becomes a startling symbol of what may be happening to our democratic principles. In *Curse of the Black Pearl*, Swann holds steadfast to his role as representative of the King in Port Royal, embracing the social hierarchy which views pirates as the piratical Other. In *Dead Man's Chest*, Swann is reduced to a puppet controlled by Beckett who manipulates Swann into signing orders and requisitions on his behalf. Beckett desires Swann's influence with the King and his pledge of allegiance to the company so Beckett can manipulate the King for his own benefit. "Every man has a price he is willing to accept," Beckett informs the

Governor, "Even for that which we never hope to sell" (*Dead Man's Chest*, 2006). So when Beckett signs the order for the arrest and subsequent hanging of Swann's daughter, Elizabeth, in response to her role in Sparrow's escape in *Curse of the Black Pearl*, Governor Swann reluctantly agrees to Beckett's demands. Swann's loyalty becomes the price he pays to ensure his daughter's safety. Yet when the Governor inquires about the value of Davy Jones's heart in *At World's End*, Beckett orders him killed. Even Swann's influence with the King is not enough to save his life. He, too, is an externality.

If the mass man's influence on cultural images, arguments posed by political parties, or manipulation of economic policies or legal loopholes fails to secure its elevated position over society, the corporation begins to construct its own legislation to be implemented by its army of masses. The army strikes from two directions: federal and state. With the influence of money on elections at all legislative levels now legitimized through the Supreme Court ruling in the *Citizens United* case, corporations are no longer bound by menial contributions such as the $2500 limit previously imposed. Now corporations are allowed to contribute infinite sums of money to political action campaigns supporting a particular political candidate. Because the donation does not go specifically to the candidate, the sky is the limit. With billions of dollars (a meager estimate) at its disposal, the mass man can now potentially buy presidential and congressional candidates and their allegiance to the imperial center.

In the 2012 election alone, as of June, 2012, CNN Money reported donors such as Sheldon Adelson, casino magnate, contributing $20 million dollars to the "Winning Our Future" superpac supporting Newt Gingrich's failed Presidential bid. Once Gingrich left the race, Adelson pledged $10 million dollars to the Romney-supporting superpac "Restore Our Future" (Riley, 2012, Website). CNN Money also revealed nine other donors including Harold Simmons, head of Contran Corporation, as contributing $11 million dollars to Karl Rove's superpac "American Crossroads," and $800,000 dollars to "Restore Our Future" (Riley, 2012). One website estimates the amount of money donated to "Restore Our Future" exceeded the $60 million dollar mark by July, 2012. Obama also has superpac support from "Priorities USA Action," with donors contributing approximately $23 million dollars to their cause. The names presented in this text include superpacs funneling exceedingly large sums of money into the 2012 Presidential election and does not include the dozens of other political action campaigns working in support of state-level candidates reflecting their ideals.

The travesty here is the process in which it has reduced political offices to a commodity to be purchased by the highest bidder. The next American President is likened to the next American Idol, with each dollar casting a vote in favor of one candidate over the other. The idol receives a recording contract. The President receives a promissory note his million-dollar donors will surely collect; it is difficult to fathom anyone donating millions of dollars to a candidate without something promised in the exchange. What will Adelson receive? What will Simmons?

Where does the economic exchange leave human beings unable to participate in such a lucrative game of chance? The tetrapus delegates humans to externalities on economic spreadsheets, collateral damage in military planning, and the masses in political and cultural acts of war. To conceal the dictate, the mass man solicits images and narratives perpetuating the severing of connections individuals share with others, images such as *Pirates of the Caribbean* and its identification of corruption as not only a human endeavor, but a specific kind of human; that kind being anyone failing to conform to the mass man's ideals. These images support attitudes of indifference, where the belief that other people's struggles are of their own making without cultural and societal influences affecting that struggle. "They" did not work hard enough; "they" are lazy because "they" do not care.

Do not ask who "they" are.

From a political perspective, the tetrapus solicits policy promoting mediocrity so the masses will view themselves as fortunate, and even powerful, when compared to those less so. This reduces the possibility of future challenges emerging from the masses no longer educated to think critically, favoring instead the average man's ability to accept conformity without question. The tetrapus is supported by political organizations such as the American Legislative Exchange Council (ALEC) which manufactures state-level legislation perpetuating a particular set of values; the organization's values *are* the corporation's values and the corporation values profit. The Huffington Post describes ALEC as "a dating service for corporate America where they set up Republican lawmakers with nice pro-business bills from good families and send them off to consummate their laws in legislatures all across the country" (Stanford, 2012, para. 3); a particularly troubling idea given that ALEC has a committee dedicated solely to issues involving education.

In the spring of 2012, the State of Georgia passed House Bill 1162, eliminating the authority local school boards possessed in relation to the establishment of charter schools in their community. That authority is now granted to the state board of education or to an external authoritative agency still answering to state board members. State Republican representatives Jan Jones, Brooks Coleman, and Edward Lindsey introduced the bill, with Jones and Lindsey being active members of ALEC and Jones a member of the ALEC education committee (Colleluori & Powell, 2012, Website). Louisiana passed a replica of Georgia's bill, requiring the construction of a charter school commission to approve or deny petitions for charter schools. Both states' legislation emulates ALEC's model education bill requiring the removal of local authority on charter school petitions. Other states discussing similar proposals as I write include Ohio, Pennsylvania, Michigan, South Carolina, and Delaware (Colleluori & Powell, 2012, Website). Even Bush, Jr. touted relations with ALEC, thanking the organization in a video presentation at ALEC's 2008 annual convention for the interaction he experienced with its members while Governor of Texas, and for their continued support of his presidency (2009, video file); ALEC praised the passage of NCLB.

If these examples are not enough to demonstrate the manipulation of the Kraken's symbolic creed for the benefit of the mass man, let us briefly explore one more element: the influence of FIDUROD epistemologies in school settings. Joe Kincheloe introduced the concept "as an acronym for the basic features of a contemporary mechanistic epistemology that is used sometimes unconsciously to shape the knowledge that permeates Western and Western-influenced cultures" (2010, p. 22). Based on historical interpretations of positivism, individuals who embrace FIDUROD have a propensity to love particular methods that isolate objective information into snippets of decontextualized data which are then further disaggregated and used to make generalized decisions about policies such as those dominating educational discourse, while influencing cultures in schools and the people dwelling within these institutions. Educational policy-makers intent on pledging allegiance to FIDUROD demonstrate their love for the rules which this particular method is ideologically attached and seek out those teachers who will not question FIDUROD's epistemological constraints to employ.

What immediately comes to mind is Erich Fromm's depiction of Adolf Eichmann, Hitler's "architect" to the events occurring during the Holocaust. Fromm identifies Eichmann as the quintessential bureaucrat; that he loved rules and only regretted the two times in his life when he disobeyed them. Fromm reports: "Eichmann did not send the hundreds of thousands of Jews to their deaths because he hated them; he neither hated nor loved anyone. Eichmann 'did his duty'" (1976, p. 151). Because his passions lie in the act of following orders, Eichmann was indifferent to humanity and to the lives he condemned to death. Eichmann's mirror image in the pirate trilogy is Beckett's henchman, Mercer, who carries out the order to murder Governor Swann and other identified externalities in the films so Beckett's hands may appear free of blood. But unlike Jones and his crew, whose corruption cannot be contained by empire and thus experiences a monstrous mutation, Mercer's acts of violence remain protected from Empire's interpretation of corruption, and so his appearance remains intact. The only image revealing Mercer's callous disregard for human life beyond his own is the reflection of hatred emerging out of his cold, dead eyes. This is perhaps why the films fail to provide a close-up of Mercer. He remains lurking in the background; rarely visible, yet always there.

Individual teachers do not have at their disposal hundreds of thousands of students to destroy, and none, I also hope, would even harbor such destructive intentions towards their students. Eichmann, mind you, did not either, although Mercer appears to have embraced the idea. But when the rules set forth by FIDUROD influence the entire sect of educational institutions, bleeding into the larger culture and society, and teachers fail to challenge these policies, then collectively we are talking about hundreds of thousands of children whose imagination and epistemological curiosities are being slaughtered each and every school day. Children become the externalities on a data analysis spreadsheet to be disaggregated by school personnel. This destruction does not require blatant acts of mass human annihilation such as those Eichmann orchestrated, isolated acts of individual assaults at the hands of Mercer, or risks analyses conducted by corporations such as General Motors to determine how many people it willingly subjects to car fires before costs interfere with profits, nor does it require conscious acts by teachers. Rather, the destruction thrives on the subtle acts of indifference to individual student needs. The death becomes the death of care, compassion or concern for the Other; the death of the human spirit. Are these not similar conditions Gasset detailed in his evolution of a hypothetical mass man?

Fromm warns us of the consequences of indifference and his words are worth quoting at length. He states:

> I am not saying that all bureaucrats are Eichmanns...Yet there are many Eichmanns among the bureaucrats, and the only difference is that they have not had to destroy thousands of people. But when the bureaucrat in a hospital refuses to admit a critically sick person because the rules require that the patient be sent by a physician, that bureaucrat acts no differently than Eichmann did. Neither do the social workers who decide to let a client starve, rather than violate a certain rule in their bureaucratic code...Once the living human being is reduced to a number, the true bureaucrats can commit acts of utter cruelty, not because they are driven by cruelty of a magnitude commensurate to their deeds, but because they feel no human bond to their subjects (1976, p. 151).

This is why an indifferent teacher is a dangerous teacher. She neither loves nor hates her students. She does her duty, submits her lesson plans on the appropriate day and adheres to the pacing guide, advancing to the next standard because the district orders her to do so even though she knows her students are not ready. She acts exactly like the bureaucrats in Fromm's text. And because *No Child Left Behind* has erased the faces of students out of the educational portrait, replacing them with statistical figures needed to make *adequate* yearly progress, the indifferent teacher no longer feels the human bond which connects her to the child hiding behind that number.

This lack of acknowledgement to the conditions connecting one human to another is how Beckett is able to justify his desire to eradicate pirates from the seas. Because he loved the rules and regulations set forth by the East India Trading Company, the power and prestige associated with the title of *Lord* Cutler Beckett, he is incapable of viewing the pirates as human which the prequel to the pirate films suggests is *The Price of Freedom* (Crispin, 2011). And because his rationalization rests on the eradication of *piracy* for the benefit of empire, he detaches himself from the fact that to accomplish this bureaucratic task, he must first *murder pirates* and possibly those who sympathize with their cause. Or he sends Mercer to do the job for him, distancing himself from the violence he invoked.

The images of Beckett, the Kraken, Governor Swann, and Mercer, are important to education because they normalize indifference, making us immune to the Other. Indifference is what conceals corrupt policies and FIDUROD epistemologies, all benefitting the corporate mass man. Through concealment, we then become tempted to behave in ways counter to the love we claim to possess for our students because we fail to see the consequences to others. Our actions negate the bonds we share with humanity, and we choose the action which limits personal anxieties or completely deadens the pain associated with the loss of an ideal of what our lives could become. We lose hope. And without hope, our capacity to envision a world different from the one we now live dissipates from view.

Our hypothetical mass man recognizes hope diminishing, and his arrogance convinces him he has shattered the human spirit. The mass man hovers over humanity, waiting impatiently for the climax to occur. Engulfed in his own power, he begins to sever the masks he once manipulated for his cause. The masks, other mass men operating in support of the larger personality and as important as they believed themselves to be, are also externalities. The first mask to be shed belongs to Governor Swann, who presumably dies at the hands of Mercer; a symbolic nod to the mass man's undermining of democratic principles with the aid of legal loopholes and legislative policies, I wonder?

The next mask eliminated belongs to the Kraken. With the mass man having amassed great power, and with the masses now being conditioned for adequate existence, the imperial center now takes the shape of the human heart, with its tentacles protruding from its center muscle in the form of arteries and veins, oxygen and blood, feeding the brain particular perspectives regarding life as it pulsates through the body with each subsequent beat. Yesterday's colonial expansion of geographic land navigates its way into new directions as each individual body becomes the new geographical conquest. We each become the site of that struggle.

Then there is Mercer, destroyed by Jones who savors the moment as his tentacles penetrate every opening of Mercer's face until a firm and final snap of the neck ends his tyranny over Jones's being. Interestingly, Jones never inquires whether Mercer would like to prolong his judgment with one hundred years of service aboard *The Flying Dutchman*. I guess even monsters have their limitations. But then Jones is destroyed by Sparrow, who places a knife in the dying hands of Will Turner and subsequently stabs Jones's heart. So Turner wins the prize of immortality, but loses the time he may have spent with his beloved Elizabeth Swann. One may consider Sparrow's gesture as an act of selflessness. After all, Sparrow had decided *he* would stab the heart to gain everlasting life sailing the seas he so loved. But Sparrow has carefully weighed his options and recognizes he has nothing to lose with Turner at the helm of *The Flying Dutchman*. And if Turner is Captain of the *Dutchman*, Sparrow is not bound by the social responsibility the position entails. Sparrow is now free to explore new pathways towards the posthuman in the fourth installment of the pirate trilogy.

That leaves us with Beckett. With movie-goers potentially having been persuaded to accept Sparrow's plight for freedom, the hypothetical mass man no longer needs Beckett, whose death completes the severing of symbolic ties. The final scene of the trilogy departs with Sparrow smiling in anticipation into a future of possibilities defined within the limitations a freedom from constraints neoliberalism carefully conceals from view. We smile too, believing the "good guys" triumphed in the end.

But looks can be deceiving. For the price of three movie tickets and some popcorn, we have potentially bought Sparrow's limited interpretation of freedom, we have bought the idea that corruption is the act of individuals other than ourselves, that only humans experience these evils, and that the problems existing in culture and society, in schools and education, are problems thrust upon us instead of recognizing our own role in the process. We offer no credence to the possibility we may be exacerbating the problems ourselves. And what is so disconcerting about our smiles is how incredibly *good* we feel after we watch the films. And because we are engulfed in our own emotional high, we fail to notice the grin on the face of our hypothetical mass man who feels the cultural tides of images and ideas shifting blindly in his favor.

Our hypothetical mass man has just taken a very large gulp of water.

CHAPTER 6

PIRATES OF THE CARIBBEAN, THE HYPOTHETICAL MASS MAN, AND THE TEACHER IN BETWEEN

"Ah love, a dreadful bond. And yet...so easily severed"
-Davy Jones, 2007, in *At World's End*

"What is done out of love always takes place beyond good and evil"
-Nietzsche, 1886/2010, p. 62

THE DICHOTOMY OF GOOD AND EVIL

While our hypothetical mass man is preoccupied with his own power, we have a few pages to study the Sparrow/Jones dichotomy more closely. To assist in this exploration, I again employ the writings of Frost and Nietzsche, the former as a comparison to Sparrow/Jones and the latter as a demonstration of how the dichotomy collapses under its own weight. In so doing, we are able to understand how the hinge dividing the two characters, corruption, is itself grounded in a corrupt interpretation of living, and that we are no better off aligning ourselves with Sparrow's plight for freedom than we are with Jones. This comparison will return us to the mass man, the pirates, and the teacher who is caught in between competing narratives of morality.

Let us begin by returning to Frost's poem (*The Road Not Taken*, 2008/1874). Frost stands at an impasse, where he gazes what at first glance appears to be two divergent pathways: One well-traveled and denoted in the previous chapter to be the road taken by the masses; the other, less traveled, and presumed to be the nobler route, trespassed by those who desire to understand the world in which we live. Nietzsche would acknowledge the road Frost took was good in that it affirmed life for Frost. Indeed, his choice made *all* the difference. But Nietzsche would also consider the possibility that if Frost *only* saw two roads, then his choice could have been bad, even evil, because Frost failed to consider the entire landscape in which the divergence occurred, thus limiting the possibilities he viewed as available.

Nietzsche would then question how divergent the paths actually were, recognizing immediately how the interpretation of one road's viability depended on its juxtaposition to the other. And this question is why Nietzsche would shake his weary head at Gasset. Not because the juxtaposition might render a comparison between good and bad, which he considered to be a natural process of life, but because the juxtaposition might render a comparison between good and evil; the former representing choices that affirm one's life; the latter representing choices that deny it. And it troubled Nietzsche that others may never question the differences between the two vastly disparate conditions; a display of ignorance he believed evolving out of the conceptual transformation of how one defined "good."

At one time, the term was associated with those in positions of power and aristocracy. The rulers of society constructed a system of morality, a "master morality," based on a belief that higher classes of people, the masters, were good simply because of their social location. The lower classes, the slaves, were defined by what they were not (courageous, honorable, etc), and "bad" became defined by a lack of goodness. Since the lower classes were inherently bad, anything they did or any belief they held, no matter how noble, was also bad.

Counter to this narrative and operating simultaneously was "slave morality." Originating out of oppressed individuals, Nietzsche argued slaves came to view the same characteristics that the masters used for themselves (powerful, aristocratic, high-minded), not as good, nor even as bad, but as downright evil. Goodness became associated with the attributes slaves held in esteem amongst their immediate community (such as humility, suffering, etc.) and was defined by the absence of any qualities a priori identified as evil.

While the categories of master and slave no longer exist in the strict, historical sense, Nietzsche argues the two competing systems of morality still linger in our midst, influencing how we read and interact with the world. In contemporary settings, what is defined as "good" stems from the individual who is master of her own fate, where the positive attributes of life come before the negative, and the comparison between good and bad is made internally, independent of other's actions in determining the value of goodness. What is good is life-affirming. She is a noble being, replete with the courage and honor needed to question and understand her world.

On the other hand, those suffering from the remnants of slave morality look upon the exact same actions as being evil. They see her independent thinking as a threat to their identity and resent her for it. So they condemn the actions and beliefs she embodies as being evil in order to substantiate their own place in the world, which they now determine to be "not evil." In this case, the positive attributes of the self are *defined* by the negative; the negative comes first, making "good" a life-negating determination. Goodness, then, becomes a *reaction* to what is already constituted as evil and is born out of *ressentiment*. Nietzsche tells us, "this *need* to direct one's view outward instead of back to oneself- is the essence of *ressentiment*: in order to exist, slave morality always first needs a hostile external world" (1967a, pp. 36-37). Thus, the dichotomy of good and evil is born out of this hostility, where evil comes to define goodness by what it is not, that is, by not being associated with the noble.

To Frost, the two roads diverging appeared to be a choice between what he considered to be two viable paths (2008/1874). The choice was not made by first identifying the evils of one road to substantiate the goodness of the other. Indeed, Frost later informs his readers both paths looked equally as worn. As master of his world, Frost gazed upon the two roads and determined one to be no better than the other. He did not look outward to make his decision, and there was no vengeance and hatred or even pity to those who may have taken the more traveled path in their lifetime. He merely wanted another direction. Thus, Frost's decision took place beyond the conditions of either/or, and that placement is what made all the difference, not the decision, for both appeared to be life-affirming.

I believe freedom from the conditions of dichotomous thought is what Nietzsche is referring to when he declares "what is done out of love always takes place beyond good and evil" (2010/1886, p. 62) because this dichotomy is an embodiment of hatred and hostility. When one is free of resentment, one is less prone to react to pre-established conditions and more likely to engage in actions affirming one's existence. Frost's poem, then, is used as a contrast to the Sparrow/Jones dichotomy whose juxtaposition relies on the life-negating principles identified in good versus evil. In this dichotomy, Jones's marginalized position to Sparrow is actually read first, as the condition on which Sparrow is rendered a good pirate. Even as we align ourselves with Sparrow, our alignment is still life-negating because the entire choice is grounded in the resentment, hatred and hostility of what is already determined to be evil. And just as Frost reveals the two paths to be equal in wear and tear, when the dichotomy of Sparrow/Jones is read in the context of Nietzsche's interpretation of good and evil, Sparrow and Jones are revealed to be, not opposites, but two variations of the same life-negating principles both Nietzsche and Gasset suggest are currently informing the masses. The dichotomy on which the films are situated slowly begins to unravel.

THE MASS MAN TRUMPS THE CHRISTIAN GOD

Now let us examine the hinge dividing the two characters while simultaneously constructing their relationship. *Pirates of the Caribbean* alludes to corruption as the distinguishing feature and defines the term as any act of defiance against the corporate, imperialist agenda. This definition explains Jones's monstrous mutation because his power, granted by his immortal state, could not be contained by empire. Dictionaries, however, offer multiple meanings- some of which support the films' interpretation; all of which challenge it. For my purposes, I limit my critique to three variations. The first definition presents corruption as a debased form of a word, as was demonstrated in the social construction of the pirate as only a negative. By ignoring the trace, the construction concealed the positive attributes a pirate embodies, that of *pirao*, of getting experience. And through this negation, the choice to engage in piracy represented that which is defined as evil, condemning *all* pirate experiences as evil. Privateers and merchant sailors then became legitimized by first determining what they were not- a pirate.

But if corruption can be defined as a debased form of a word, then language is also subject to corruption. And when we blindly ingest words and their meanings without critically exploring these meanings, we not only perpetuate that corruption in our daily interaction with others, we *become* a part of that corruption. It defines us. We cease acting with others, instead merely *reacting* to what has already been established. We become dependent on the other while simultaneously denouncing their position. And we repress our knowledge of dependency because of the self-loathing it induces. Thus the catachresis, where our boundaries are potentially defined by the dichotomies we buy into. This is why Nietzsche would question whether or not Frost acknowledges the entire landscape in which the divergence between paths occurred. The poem does not reveal any such cognition, but that does not mean Frost did not have the entire scenery in his view. He may not have found it important to include in his poem. But if Frost did *not* notice his surroundings, then the choice he made may not have made *all* the difference, it may have made *no* difference because the choice was presented as either/or; either one of the two roads, or nothing, thus negating the landscape on which the divergence occurred. As in the case of Sparrow/Jones, the interpretation of good, as consequential to evil, would be made out of ignorance to the term's own corruption. And we would leave Frost's poem exactly as we left the theatre after viewing the pirate trilogy, feeling good about ourselves because we now define goodness through a corruption no longer within our periphery.

Dictionaries also define corruption as a moral perversion, depravity, or the perversion of integrity. Nietzsche would immediately raise a thickened eyebrow to this definition, not only because he understood corruption to be subjective, but also in his belief that the entire concept of morality was itself a perversion in its placement of restraints on one's will to power. There are two perspectives we may engage at this point, both reaching the same conclusion. The first is that if someone is caught inside the catachresis of slave morality and fails to question the life-negating principles constructed out of the dichotomy of good and evil, then any will to power may result in a defeat of that will because freedom would be defined strictly by the perversion of the term. Such is the case in *Pirates of the Caribbean*, where freedom is perverted to mean only a freedom from constraints and in support of neoliberal ideology. The characteristics of slave morality such as humility or the ability to suffer would not challenge the limitations on one's life, it would support them, rendering a revolt of the masses a revolt of the self while leaving the systems of oppression intact and unscathed.

From the other perspective, Nietzsche would look at the perversion as symptomatic of the Christian moral imperative in that the Christian doctrine of a suffering Christ became the symbolism of slave morality. Thus, our actions and behaviors were not really action at all but were reactions to a world now governed by the suffering embedded in "Thou shall not..." Nietzsche seized the contradiction evolving out of Christian morality in that the religion teaches "thou shall not judge." Yet, by first comparing all actions to what is already considered evil, individuals were, in effect, passing judgment and condemning those who acted counter to the Christian moral imperative. There was no affirmation of the self, only negation via the impossibility to achieve strict interpretations of goodness. Either we are evil or we are not. "Either the one is true or the other" (Nietzsche, 1967b, p. 32), because the moral imperative, the quest for divine perfection, dictates actions cannot be both.

82

Here is where questions of morality stemming out of the dichotomy of good and evil become even more compelling. If there is no slavery in the strict historical sense, and yet slave morality is still lingering in our midst, then who is the contemporary master? Certainly, Nietzsche would argue religious doctrines continue to fill that role. If he were alive today, I imagine him scribing a still scathing critique of Christianity's continued influence in the world. But how would he respond to the power amassed by our hypothetical mass man and the cohesiveness within structures of violence vibrating from an imperial center? I believe Nietzsche would argue the mass man has finally trumped the Christian God, but only by engaging the same slave morality still guiding the masses. In other words, he would argue we have merely substituted one authoritative figure for another, leaving the system of morality substantiating both idols virtually intact. We are still defining goodness through what we hate, and we still resent noble beings for their questions against systems of morality. But because we are now drenched in a culture of mediocrity, we no longer see the corruption we are perpetuating. We have *become* a part of our problem.

Nietzsche describes how, when what one values collapses, and all that one holds dear is rendered meaningless in the collapse, the potential to substitute a new reality evolves. But the substitution is still framed within the values believed to have been shed. Nothing has really changed. He tells us,

> The nihilistic question 'for what?' is rooted in the old habit of supposing that the goal must be put up, given, demanded *from outside*- by some *superhuman authority*. Having unlearned faith in that, one still follows the old habit and seeks another authority that can speak unconditionally and command goals and tasks. (1967b, p. 16)

Even though we may have denounced slave morality, and perhaps even God, the need to define our actions as good is still viewed outwardly. Our habits have not changed. Our hypothetical mass man, having been granted unconditional authority from the masses to speak on their behalf, fills the role now vacated by the Christian God. He becomes a substitute that manipulates the limited interpretation of morality in public spaces, allowing for other mass-man personalities to crush dialogue through verbal assaults on those deemed evil. He conceals the relationship humans have with each other through a pedagogy of indifference which teaches the value of self-interests by devaluing social justice.

Here, in the context of our space and time, the definition of good becomes intertwined with elements of master *and* slave morality as courageous becomes an attribute assigned to those who speak out on behalf of the masses, against the noble, and at the expense of the oppressed. And the suffering of others becomes the necessary evil needed to sustain one's own social location. All of which operate to sustain our hypothetical mass man who numbs our reaction to this suffering by convincing us that oppression is something others have *chosen* to experience. But there is no internal attribution of good and bad. We still look outward, to our mass man, for directions on how to react.

What is of further interest is how the rhetoric associated with the 2012 Republican primaries, a political party which celebrates its relationship with Christianity, alludes to the supplanting of the Christian God with this pejorative figure. Divine perfection has been substituted with imperial and corporate perfection which may only be achieved through our limited role as consumer. Profit margins, higher dividends, and exorbitant bonuses become the new alter of worship. And the mass man is heralded as the new "Creator" of all things because he creates jobs. This is an interesting evolution of the mass man because Gasset believed him incapable of producing anything new. Rather, he was the ultimate consumer, devouring all that noble beings had created. Now he sends his disciples, his zombie politicians whose appearance remains intact because they support the corporate agenda, to rid the world of the evils of independent thought. What he has created is a desire in others to consume more.

Nietzsche once called the transformation of "good," from its comparison with bad to its comparison with evil, as a "creative turn" in that slaves had inverted the meaning of goodness into its opposite and normalized the conditions of hatred. I believe what we are witnessing today is a "decisive turn," where goodness is no longer being strictly defined through its *inversion*, but also through a *diversion* away from an Other. Characteristics defining master morality such as nobility are still condemned, but they have joined forces with the characteristics slave morality once applauded (such as the ability to suffer and to remain humble in hostile conditions). These attributes are now identified as the "necessary evil" believed to be embodied in the lower class. But because this suffering is now viewed as a choice citizens of this social stature have made for themselves, the desire of the more privileged classes to assist these individuals has decreased substantially, for neoliberal ideology presses the question of why anyone would want to assist those who do not help themselves, as if poverty and deprivation was a lucrative choice to be made. This social stratum is no longer viewed in comparison to the powerful and aristocratic who may not "see" these individuals at all, but situated in direct opposition to a middle class of people who feel the social pressures from above *and* below. The new motto is "Every man for himself," or the paralyzing "If you're not with us then you're against us." The dichotomy of good and evil still reign's supreme, but those deemed evil have quadrupled in numbers. The resentment is not only felt towards the proverbial "have's" of the world, but also to the "have-nots," where any assistance to their existence such as government subsidy programs including welfare, healthcare, medicare, and public schooling is criticized for diverting funds away from programs directly benefitting the masses; programs such as those in support of the military and in protection of a mutated interpretation of freedom. Indifference is the new norm. And this decisive turn is a perversion of both systems of morality. Corruption is no longer the exception; it's the rule.

CONDITIONS OF THE HEART

From the previous interpretations, we learn how corruption infiltrates the broad cultural systems of language and morality. The words we use to name our world and the systems of morality helping to construct our interpretation of these names leads to the final definition discussed in this text: corruption is an act, an engagement of behavior. *Pirates of the Caribbean* implies corruption to be an act of defiance against imperialism; the action is a choice we make for ourselves. However, if we apply this definition to the broader culture in which the film is situated, a problem reflecting the fallibility of the films' own situated-ness within the dichotomy of good and evil arises.

In the case of the pirates of Somalia, they are determined to be corrupt by a Western perspective steeped in imperial linguistic and cultural codifications. Their defiance is against trans-national corporations intent on exploiting ecological and non-governmental, but by no means anarchical, conditions. The act of corruption is the resurgence of piracy and this act binds Somali pirates to their predecessors. Sanders writes of Bartholomew Roberts, heralded as the greatest pirate to ever "go on the account", that he "and other pirates of the Golden Age owe their bloodthirsty reputation to one fact...they stole from Englishmen" (2007, p. 245). If we utilize Bakon's definition of the corporation as the "large Anglo-American publicly traded business" (2004, p. 3) whose own predecessor, the East India Company, operated at its height during the same time period, then the only difference between historical pirates and contemporary pirates is which country representing imperialism was being defied, not the act itself. Both are rendered corrupt by the same Western perspective which sought, and still seeks, to define the term.

But if the pirate trilogy's definition is to be believed, then the entire foundation on which the United States is built is also corrupt. When John Adams warned of the possible erection of a U.S. empire, he revealed his intent to defy British imperialism. The Boston Tea Party and the ensuing revolution were the acts of corruption. The constitution, Bill of Rights, and the cultural constructions evolving out of that defiance were framed within that corruption. What did our founding fathers steal? They stole the right to define the terms of one's own existence. And this freedom is the same freedom both historical and contemporary pirates sought as well. Yet one is considered corrupt while the other is considered a superpower. One is scorned while the other celebrated. And this difference is why the films' allusion to corruption as an act and as a choice one makes for oneself borders on the absurd because no one (that I am aware) willingly *chooses* to be corrupt. *Pirates of the Caribbean* assumes a universal meaning of the term, oblivious to the fact that many identify the corruption to be imperialism itself. And while we may defy imperial authoritarianism, it is *through* corruption that we reclaim the sense of freedom achieved by the pirates *and* our founding fathers. Our quest for freedom is an act of love because we use our interpretation of the term to engage in life-affirming decisions. Our action is not defined by what is evil but by an informed determination to strive towards individual wills to power. We choose life, we learn, we grow; we become what we strive to Become with the process acting recursively as new aspirations evolve.

The greatest corruption celebrated in the pirate trilogy, then, is not corruption per se for that is subjective, but in the choice made leading up to that corruption. The choice is a condition of the heart to which we are all privy -for Jones chose love. But even this fact does not distinguish him from Sparrow because Sparrow chose love, too. He loved himself; the ultimate egoist perusing the sea in search of immortality. Not to suggest Jones is the antithetical altruist, but because his love was for an Other, he was incapable of indifference to that Other- at least initially, for his love soon mutated into extreme conditions of hatred and hostility. And this fact represents the contradiction in the films, with the dichotomy of Sparrow/Jones ultimately collapsing under its own weight and the hinge of corruption not distinguishing between the two characters but revealing their similarities; a frightening revelation in its glorification of indifference.

At one time, Jones loved the Sea Goddess, Calypso. Little is revealed of their relationship other than allusions to its intensity. But the repercussions of love are a major plot in the Pirate trilogy. Presumably upon his death, Calypso petitions Jones to captain *The Flying Dutchman*. In his immortal state, Jones could embrace a world of "in-between," not fully dead, but not fully human either. For every ten years of service, Jones would be rewarded with one day on land to reunite with his love. During that time period, Jones dedicated himself to the cause, ferrying those who died at sea "to the other side" (2007, *At World's End*). He cared for them, respected their anxiety when being confronted with the uncertainty "in-between" often accompanies. But this is secondary to the indifference prominent in the films; the promise of love is erased by its perils.

When the day comes for Jones to reunite with Calypso, she fails to show. Enraged by her rejection, Jones falls into a trajectory of callous disregard for those he once offered compassion. No longer concerned with his social responsibility, Jones's appearance evolves into a monstrosity. But the mutation affectively symbolizing his corruption was *not* Jones's choice. Rather, it was a consequence of him *choosing* to intimately connect with another. The rage he felt towards Calypso upon her rejection led to a life of hostility; a reactive force dependent upon Calypso's actions which Jones came to view as evil. When he betrays her by manipulating others to bind her into human form, Jones not only cuts Calypso off from her beloved sea, he cuts himself off from that which had come to define him, leaving behind a shallow shell of an individual no longer capable of love through which his indifference evolved.

If there *is* a difference between Sparrow and Jones, it is the fact that Sparrow is presented to always be indifferent, thus no mutation was experienced as the indifference had always defined his existence. *This* is the corruption celebrated in the films, teaching us that it is better to avoid the risks of love rather than engage them. When we choose indifference, we negate love's risks because we no longer care about them. bell hooks argues when faced with rejection, our reaction may be to sever the relational ties to that love (2000). Our reaction is to run. Jones's response is much more severe. He literally cuts out his heart and places it in an empty chest, much like his already vacuous soul, to sever the pain of rejection. Instead of a symbol for all we may love in society, Jones becomes an admonition of it, representing all that we loathe. Herein lays the miseducation of Davy Jones. Because his definition of love was always contingent on an external, super-human authority (remember, as the Sea Goddess, Calypso had to be *bound* in human form, suggesting she previously embodied some transcendental form), he was already defining love from outside of himself. So when Calypso failed to rendezvous with him, love became associated with evil. For Jones, love was easily severed because it was never really love at all but a tenderized version of the hatred and hostility he already possessed of the world. Hence, this love was already a negation of his life; his mutation was a result of his no longer caring about the negation.

Yet, when I reflect on my life and career as a teacher, caught between the historical pirates of long ago and a hypothetical mass man intent on defining the cultural and societal conditions I have regarding freedom, I cannot help but feel a certain kinship with Jones. I believe as teachers, we are being asked to cut out our hearts in hopes of severing the connections we feel towards our students, our colleagues, and ourselves. With the institution of education, heavily influenced by the conditions of mediocrity, swayed by the lure of profits associated with privatized public education where corporations are legally bound to increase dividends at the expense of the people involved, and motivated to erase corruption from the institution by burdening teachers with these evils through the connection between salaries and test scores, the children entrusted in our care are propelled further into the background. How much longer will we be able to even glimpse sight of their silhouettes?

Obama's *Race to the Top* initiative wields statistics like a weapon of mass destruction, threatening us with termination of employment should we begin thinking for ourselves. As a result of this fear, we cease acting in ways conducive to the love we once possessed for our students and begin reacting to our own fears. We cut out our hearts to deaden the pain associated with the rejection of the idea of what we believed education *should* be. Thus, the miseducation of Davy Jones becomes our own miseducation because our reactions, no matter how "good" we may interpret them to be, are already life-negating in their reliance on the external forces constructing the conditions for that love. We have been conditioned to define goodness through its evil opposite, and the love we once embodied slowly mutates into indifference because we internalize the idea that a lack of caring and compassion is the only way to deal with our anxieties. Our physical appearance remains intact because our indifference supports the corporate, imperial agenda, but our mental faculties have now turned against us. The mutation may not be visible, but our hearts know a change is evolving.

A dear friend dedicating thirty years of service to elementary-age schoolchildren recently confided that we cannot do anything about testing in schools. She believes the oppression to be a permanent state of being. In this reality, she has chosen to teach her students "the best way I can." Her choice, she says, is based on her love for them. Unfortunately, this is not an action of love but a reaction reflecting defeat leading to indifference. My friend's resignation to the policies preying upon her vulnerability does not restore the humanity being stripped away with each subsequent test question or the next, potentially more malicious educational policy. No, my friend's complacency in the area of testing is perpetuating the very system of oppression she denounces. Yet because she has accepted the conditions of testing, she offers no substantial challenge to the conditions. She does not see the contradiction in her own words. In her blindness, she whole-heartedly believes she is working diligently for her students, oblivious to the fact that her work is negating the love she claims through its negation of her students' capacity to grow beyond the limitations of learning celebrated in school policies. And what is so disconcerting is that she is not alone in her beliefs. She is one of many who have chosen silence as their best recourse.

In 1999, David Purpel outlined the moral outrage he felt regarding the institution of education, telling us, "As educators our responsibility is surely not to carry out current educational policies and practices...but to uphold and nourish the cherished principles that inform our deepest dreams and aspirations" (p. 69). Not that Purpel was asking teachers to ignore their contractual obligations to the state; he was not advocating for educational anarchy. Rather, in our role as educators, Purpel was asking for consideration as *to what* or *to whom* we were responding in that role. For if we choose the state, our response negates the people involved in the curricular process. And that response, again, no matter how noble we believe it to be, negates life rather than affirms it.

Purpel further suggested "This is a time when we need to talk less about our educational goals and more about our moral aspirations, less about our professional role as educators and more about ethical responsibilities as citizens" (1999, p. 69). As ethical citizens, we are to teach others how to become masters of their own world as opposed to slaves in a world others have constructed *for* them. But the current conditions inundated by the demands of our hypothetical mass man and his neoliberal bedfellows have annihilated dialogue and manipulated systems of morality to the point that any resistance to what *we* may view as corrupt is itself re-presented as that corruption. In the process, we have succumbed to what Diane Ravitch suggests is the loss of "our outrage, even our ability to care" (2012, website, para. 13). Ravitch implores us to reject the new normal of mass teacher firings, high-stakes testing, and the culture of fear accompanying these policies. The new normal is Sparrow, a whimsical representation of indifference whose goodness is defined by the evils he is not. And the conditions of the new normal are a question of values Ravitch believes cannot be challenged from a position of indifference. As teachers, we must reclaim our outrage and discern where our loyalties lie. For if our loyalties are to the policies perpetuating the negation of learning and individual student growth, then our efforts are not towards curricular reformation perpetuating life-affirming lessons with the young, but to educational deformation perpetuating the life-negating standards of the masses, and thus the mass man. I cannot speak for others, but perpetuating educational deformation is not where my heart resides.

Look at where Freire situates his loyalties in relation to a *Pedagogy of the Heart*:

My radical posture requires of me an absolute loyalty to all men and women. An economy that is incapable of developing programs according to human needs, and that coexists indifferently with the hunger of millions of people to whom everything is denied, does not deserve my respect as an educator. (1997, p. 36)

It is difficult to speak of absolutes in a postmodern world where meaning is contingent on the context in which it is read. But Freire states with unwavering resolve that his loyalties lie with people, with the human beings involved in the educational process. He rejects the idea that policies and procedures cannot somehow reflect the love shared between humans to thwart indifference, arguing that to support this belief would be fatalistic. Perhaps this is why he felt the need to preface where his loyalties reside as a radical posture, a radical love.

One's culture has a propensity to ostracize anything associated with radicalness. Freire himself was exiled for a time resulting from his "radical" departure of supporting policies perpetuating indifference. In a presentation given at Georgia Southern University in 2009, Shirley Steinberg spoke of Joe Kincheloe and the radical love he possessed for his students. Kincheloe devoted countless hours conferencing and questioning doctoral candidates to ensure an understanding of the complexities existing between institutional education, cultural norms and societal laws, and how they manifests themselves in classroom spaces. These hours were not dedicated to indoctrinating others into his personal beliefs but to encourage students to develop and articulate their own ideas from a broad spectrum of philosophies. He was encouraging nobility where, as in Freire's teachings, individuals may learn to read the oppressions they experience in the context of their own lives. And also like Freire, Kincheloe was exiled, not in the geographical sense, but in the hatred Steinberg suggested some of his colleagues felt towards him. He held no blind allegiance to the masses, thus he was perceived as a threat.

In relation to radical love, Kincheloe describes how he arose every morning excited about the possibilities presented when searching for new insights into the world, calling it a "'great wide open' with yet unimagined possibilities for the remaking of selfhood and socio-political relationships" (2010, p. 179). In many ways, Kincheloe embodied the pirate in his rejection of being defined by the same societal norms perpetuating the social injustices he advocated against. I can picture him aboard the deck of a pirate ship, standing alongside Freire as both cast a lingering gaze on the open sky dreaming of a world that could be; as Freire argued, "it is impossible to live without dreams" (2007, pp. 3-4). Was this not a similar dream of pirates? Was this not a similar dream of John Adams? Is this not a similar dream of ours? And yet, does this not speak to the heart of our struggles as teachers, caught in between the impossibility of living *without* dreams and our hypothetical mass man's desire for us *not* to live *with* them? Dreaming is dangerous; if we dare to dream, we may come to realize our potential in carrying these dreams to fruition through our actions rather than merely existing in a perpetual state of reaction.

Sure, we may be perceived as radical, as corrupt, dare I say, as a pirate, but at least our moral outrage and indignation to indifference may have a positive effect on the students entrusted in our care. And is that not another common reason offered as to why we choose to enter the field of education, because we want to make a difference in the life of another? The time has come for us to articulate loud and clear what kind of difference we wish to make and how we define our love for students. For merely stating that we possess love is no longer a sufficient reason, if it ever was. Indeed, this claim is just as vacuous as Davy Jones's chest cavity. Do we define love in relation to life-affirming conditions of goodness a priori to what is perceived as bad? Or do we limit our understanding of love to an a posteriori identification grounded on the life-negating concept of evil? This question speaks to the heart of the catachresis, for any response we offer will be perceived by *someone* as being corrupt. And if I am going to be designated as corrupt by the masses holding dogmatically to a dichotomy of good and evil, then I intend to embrace the pirate already within me. I intend to live, learn, and teach with a pedagogy of passion and purpose befitting a teacher-as-pirate. In so doing, I re-position myself in classroom spaces as teacher-as-subject, dropping anchor amidst a sea of lived experiences evolving out of relationships built *with* my students and *with* others.

Gosse once called pirates cowardly, but I believe it takes more courage to embrace the "yet unimagined possibilities" (Kincheloe, 2010, p. 179) than it does to erase them. Whether we choose to hold steadfast to the cultural construction of pirates as only negative beings or embrace their quest for freedom as a possibility offered in contemporary settings, we may find common ground in the fact that historical pirates were passionate people striving for the restoration of humanity for those brave enough to board the ship, and this passion is what distinguishes them from the indifference they experienced while serving as legitimate merchant seamen. Sanders informs how "There can be no doubt Bartholomew Roberts was responsible for a greater quantity of human suffering during his career as a [legitimate] slaver than his career as a pirate" (2007, p. 245). How much human suffering are *we* responsible for in our denial of youth oppressions resulting from a culture of fear and high-stakes testing shrouding schools today? How many wounds have *we* inflicted through our silent acquiescence to the culture of cruelty exemplified in educational environments? What *more* must our hypothetical mass man *do* before we finally decide to rekindle our own desire in making a *positive* difference? As we contemplate this question, we must also inquire as to what is holding us back. We may look to the pirate code for this answer. For its greatest treasure is identified in what the code reveals about us as educators.

TRACES OF LOVE IN A PIRATE CODE

In describing the world of piracy, Sanders asserts "there is an emotional intensity to pirate life that seeps through the dry, contemporary accounts" (2007, p. 80); stories constructing a dehumanized and delegitimized image of the pirate-as-object to be written while simultaneously erasing pirate passions and intensity in the account. As teachers, we experience the dry, contemporary accounts written about us which dehumanizes our efforts, reducing us as objects to be exploited in similar fashion as historical pirates. These accounts do not enhance our passions. They anesthetize us, numbing our passions until we feel nothing at all. In chronicling the life of Bartholomew Roberts, Sanders contends "At a distance of three hundred years

Roberts is a morally ambiguous figure- a thief, certainly, a killer, occasionally, but never the ruthless cut-throat of pirate myth" (2007, p. 244). At a distance of three hundred years, how will others chronicle today's teacher? As a thief, certainly not, unless one considers stealing moments of authentic learning for our students an act of thievery; as a killer, perhaps, depending on how one chooses to define death. But maybe, just maybe, we will be studied for the ruthless intensity that seeps through the dry accounts of teacher-as-failing object as we embrace the passions needed to challenge the corrupt interpretations of learning we are expected to perpetuate. When living, learning, and teaching at the level of intensity passion invokes, love is not as easily severed as Jones would have us believe. No, intensity binds us together as whole subjects, humanized beings, whose love for the promise of a socially-just world offers opportunities to counter the myriad oppressions we experience. It is a love "beyond good and evil" (Nietzsche, 2010/1886), where its conditions set the stage for all experiences yet to come, interpreted through individual wills to power. And this love represents the weakest point in the hypothetical mass man's DNA but the strongest point in ours. For unlike a corporation personified, we, as humans, possess the capacity to engage in Freire's radical love.

hooks asserts, "to truly love we must learn to mix various ingredients- care, affection, recognition, respect, commitment, and trust, as well as honest and open communication" (2000, p. 5). When any one of the ingredients is excluded, our capacity to love becomes increasingly difficult. For hooks, love should be read as a verb and not merely as an emotional response. The latter limits one's capacity to love as something received, as a *reaction* dependent on the actions of another rather than its own independent event; thus, it is not really love at all. And our reactions perpetuate the dichotomy of good/evil. Recognizing loyalty as a condition of radical love, we must include the concept in the list of ingredients. hooks will not object to this inclusion because both she and Freire speak of a commitment towards others and to individual and collective liberations from oppression. Taken together, these two authors help form the basis for my interpretation of radical love, informing what I present in the next chapter as outlaw pedagogy. Suffice it to say at this juncture that outlaw pedagogy is firmly situated in the passionate and the purposeful.

Freire explains "The passion with which I know, I speak, or I write does not, in any way, diminish the commitment with which I announce or denounce. I am a totality and *not a dichotomy*" (1997, p. 30, emphasis added). In his pronouncement, Freire defies arbitrary conditions of either/or by defining himself as a whole person. There are not two distinct personalities residing within one body where he is faced with the choice of wearing one mask for the workplace and another for his most intimate friends. No, his love exists beyond the conditions of either/or, engaging the lived experience with his entire body at all times in his life. Freire's statement does not negate the oppressions he has lived and witnessed; on the contrary, his capacity to radically love the world, the good *and* the bad, provides him the strength to confront his oppressions and anxieties. To be passionate is to be active, and activity is what he shares in common with Bartholomew Roberts.

Coincidentally, Roberts' greatest heist was off the coast of Recife, Brazil, where two centuries later the great educator would be born. Roberts would gain recognition and respect from requiring any pirate who sailed under his command to sign an article of agreement, a pirate code, in protection of individual rights while on the account. Freire would gain recognition by writing a text articulating a pedagogy worthy of educators to teach and live by, in protection of those elements promoting a socially-just and inclusive society in which all people are provided opportunities to learn and grow.

The pirate code served mainly to protect crew members from the captain predation many experienced while sailing as legitimate merchant seamen and to establish equal distribution of goods with ramifications included to those who appropriated more than their fair share. There were strict penalties for bringing women aboard ship or the assault of any woman imprisoned on board. The code restricted the abuse of alcohol and gambling, with all disagreements aboard ship to be settled on land. There were stipulations on the amount earned for those who were wounded in battle and could no longer fight, as well as repercussions for those who were ill-prepared for that battle.

But like all fledgling forms of democracy (the pirate code has been considered to be a prototype of this ideology), the code was not devoid of weaknesses. There is evidence to support an exclusion of some pirates based on racial differences. Jeffrey Bolster argues:

> Bold black seamen joined disgruntled white soldiers, sailors, and servants confederating as pirates along sun-drenched Caribbean sea-lanes. Contemptuous of the authority that had always repressed them...these 'desperate rogues' created an egalitarian, if ephemeral, social order that rejected imperial society's hierarchy and forced labor (1997, p. 13).

Bolster's summation alludes to the connection pirates felt in relation to class; a relation able to transcend racial boundaries on particular vessels where the promise of freedom increased substantially for a black man escaping slavery. Unfortunately, because we have no pirate history beyond what others have written, it is difficult to surmise how racial equality aligned with contemporary proclamations of pirate democracies.

As a result of this uncertainty, I am reluctant to share in the claim that pirate ships represented potential democratic places because pirates tended to define democracy in terms of limitations relating strictly to decision-making processes. Perhaps one may conclude there was an effort to embrace *some* form of democracy when compared to the lack thereof experienced on land, but only insofar as the captain interpreting the pirate code chose to include sailors other than those of European descent as part of the crew. Roberts' crew was inclusive, as was Blackbeard's, Captain Kidd's, and several others. But Captain Edward Low refused to give credence to black sailors and is reported by Bolster to have enslaved any who attempted to board his ship. Thus, the democratic principles associated with piracy were always framed within a white, male, European lens. And the representation of pirate democracies built solely on the equal participation of voting and prize distributions demonstrates our own limited view of democracy. As Paul Carr argues, "The mere act of voting does not make a democracy" (2011, p. 50). Rather, it makes a limitation of democracy where broader, more inclusive modes of social justice are excluded from the conversation because we all presumably share an equal right to vote. Perhaps this limitation is why Marcus Rediker suggests "seamen who became pirates escaped from one closed system only to find themselves encased in another" (1987, p. 279), for they failed to account how their own beliefs such as racial inequalities existing between some white pirates and the institution of slavery had already been codified within the system of language brought with them when they boarded the ship.

Nevertheless, there *was an attempt* made by those such as Roberts to relieve some of the oppressions pirates felt on land by attempting to restore their humanity through the pirate code; a restoration Freire argues is crucial to the educational process. Through this restoration, the *promise* of freedom reappeared to those who boarded Roberts' ship. And while the racial demographics remain questionable in relation to pirate democracies, the code did provide inclusion into a system attempting to transcend class boundaries experienced on land.

Recall Spivak's definition of critical as a limit to knowing. The limitation of race or gendered inclusion in the world of seventeenth-century piracy may serve as an entry point into the twenty-first century world of teacher-as-pirate. How may we work to become more inclusive in our teachings? One pathway is to liberate ourselves from the idea that pirates were only negative beings so that we may expose the pirate already within us via *pirao*. By placing the previous limitations at the forefront of all choices to follow, we begin the process of thinking like a pirate. When we think like a pirate, recognizing how power systems of closure intersect and coincide with subaltern desires to open these systems for questioning, then we glimpse sight of one aspect Rediker suggests the code invoked: a fierce loyalty to each other (1987). When we think like a pirate, we see the world as a piratical place which must be understood in its piracy. I believe pirates want to be understood for their loyalties connecting one to another in the collective ethos of a radical love demonstrated in response to that loyalty, and to be seen as contradictory to an indifferent world which so easily cast them aside.

According to Rediker, pirates viewed themselves as mutual "risk-sharing partners" (p. 264) who "valued and respected the skills of their comrades" (p. 263). This respect extended out from the pirate code which worked towards humanizing individuals who saw in their fellow shipmates equality in relation to the actions transpiring onboard pirate vessels. This respect included other vessels as it was rare to engage in combat with other pirates who also shared a subjugation as the piratical Other. The code was a common thread weaving throughout all of pirate life requiring respect in the mutual exchange to those who embraced its symbolism. For a group of individuals not recognized as having morals, they certainly reflected a mastery of individual and collective wills to power.

Teachers, too, have a code: an article of agreement we sign upon acceptance of employment to embark on a voyage of the ship we call classroom spaces. We eagerly sign our agreement to uphold the policies and procedures passed down from school and district level personnel. K-12 teacher contracts in Georgia require an oath to "go on the account" 190 days a year, attend meetings, to be on our posts in a timely manner, and to refrain from engaging in behaviors detrimental to students or to the school. But unlike the pirate code working to protect pirates, teacher contracts protect the state. In Georgia's contract of employment, there are stipulations as to how salary will be assigned to teachers with these stipulations becoming null if the state is unable to meet salary demands. This has been exemplified in the number of furlough days teachers have received over the last few years in relation to Georgia's economic struggles. Teachers are contracted with the district and not individual schools, so even though they interview and are hired by a particular school, there is no guarantee the teacher will actually teach in that environment. She may be reassigned at the discretion of district-level administrators.

These stipulations appear reasonable even though they firmly protect state interests. What is interesting is the requirements of teachers to "obey such reasonable rules and regulations as may from time to time be put in force..." (2006, Georgia Contract of Agreement). Similar to my prior use of the term, "reasonable" is also subjective, granted its signification by the reader interpreting its meaning within the context offered while being influenced by the reader's individual lived experience. Therefore, teachers who choose to be loyal to students instead of the policies dictating the time we spend in classrooms may do so under the *reasonable* assertion that the policies require *unreasonable* attention to tests and measurements which fail miserably in their attempt to educate children in understanding the complex world in which we live. A pirate would read these conditions and surmise that just because we sign a contract with the state *does not also mean we pledge our loyalties*. Like Freire, our loyalties should always be to our students and others - that is, to the *people* involved in the educational process *even when that loyalty pits us against the state*. In today's culture of cruelty exemplified in the testing mantra, my fear is that too many teachers are abandoning ship, losing sight of the most common reasons cited by undergraduate students as a reason for entering the profession: The love of children and a desire to make a difference. They are potentially denying that love and loyalty by responding to the dictates of the state. And they do not question how their love is defined.

Another colleague shared with me a memorandum distributed to the faculty and staff of the Griffin-Spalding County School District in Griffin, Georgia. In this memorandum, the Superintendent of schools stated "Sometimes we're so committed to one another that we let that personal loyalty win over our *loyalty* to the system" (Jones, 2012, Website). The memorandum was in response to a personnel hearing in which the Superintendent was accused of sexually harassing a teacher in the system. The Superintendent was cleared of any wrongdoing but nevertheless felt the need to "clarify" the system's stance on loyalty. As a value, Griffin-Spalding

County Schools define loyalty as support for "public education, our school system, our schools, and each other. We care for our students- they are why we are here" (2012, Website). But this care was undermined by the Superintendent's clarification that personal loyalties should not supersede one's loyalties *to the system*; system needs come first. Where does that leave students? According to the district's own definition, students register dead last in its hierarchy of loyalties. But just because the Superintendent views system loyalty as supreme does not also mean we, as teachers, must internalize and abide by this view. And we cannot let these kinds of statements thwart our responsibility to our students. We must speak out against these claims and raise questions regarding their intentions.

William Ayers refers to loyalty as a question of moral commitment, telling us:

> I want teachers to figure out what they are teaching *for*, and what they are teaching *against*. I want to teach against oppression and subjugation, for example, and against exploitation, unfairness, and unkindness, and I want others to join me in that commitment. I want to teach toward freedom, for enlightenment and awareness, wide-awakeness, protection of the weak, cooperation, generosity, and love. (2004, p. 18)

Teaching towards freedom is a whole-body experience only achieved when we place students at the forefront of their own educational experience. This means retrieving them from their hiding place behind the statistical figures used to determine how well they adapt to mediocrity.

Reflecting on Ayer's commitment to the human condition, I cannot help but place it in the context of the Pirate trilogy. In *At World's End*, prior to the climactic battle between Beckett and the pirates, Sparrow and the others recognize they are severely outnumbered. As some of the crew petition to abandon the cause which will certainly lead to their demise, Elizabeth Swann storms above the crowd, commands their ears, and shouts in their direction: If we will not die for freedom, *"then what shall we die for?"* (2007). While teaching itself is not a question of life or death, the moral commitment Ayers asks us to make, the loyalties to people Freire articulates, and the love hooks advocates may be viewed in a similar context. What shall we, as teachers, work for? Is it truly the policies and procedures attempting to control our actions? I sincerely hope not. Because if our passions lie in perpetuating policy over people, to borrow a phrase from Chomsky, then what we are working for *is* a matter of death: the death of the human spirit.

These acts and the conditions and behaviors they solicit, in Freire's terms, are not worth my respect both as an educator and as a human being. As a teacher, I work with a pedagogy of passion and purpose, intent on perpetuating the radical love Freire advocates in his work with the fierce loyalty of a pirate to improving the conditions of and with humanity. When I view current educational and cultural conditions in which we live and work through the eyes of a pirate, then I have no choice but to reject these conditions and their hindrance on my commitment towards the *promise* of a freedom each of us defines for ourselves. This is not a statement regarding the return of rugged individualism, for any freedom worth fighting for, and yes, worth dying for, may only be achieved while working collectively through and against our struggles with oppression. When I view these same conditions through the untold stories of Somali pirates, then I must resist the limitations imposed on my actions, embracing my heart and its capacity to love as an opening of the catachrestic boundaries structured before, around, and within me. I must commit, not to shallow, unreasonable policies and procedures perpetuating indifference, but to the *people* with whom this Earth and our voyages are shared. I commit, then, with the passions and intensity of my predecessors, to being/Becoming...a pirate.

This commitment, however, is not a license for anything goes. Like Purpel, I am not advocating for educational anarchy. But as Sanders argued in relation to Roberts' experiences, there was a degree of organization observed while aboard pirate ships. This prevented the chaos culturally constructed of pirate life. While they did reject the laws of the land perpetuating class oppressions, that rejection did not prevent them from instilling laws and norms within their own culture as a pathway to preventing anarchy from occurring; the laws were instilled to promote life, not deny it. As teachers, we are not privy to constructing laws governing our actions, but we *are* in a position to challenge these laws and the cultural norms coinciding with that construction. We *are* capable of discerning which laws reflect corrupt interpretations of learning. And we *are* fully adept at thwarting the erasure of that corruption from an institution determined to delineate all of the cultural "blame" in our laps by perpetuating the image of the teacher-as-failing.

In making the case for what he considers to be the inevitable "fall" of the U.S. empire, Galtung asserts all empires "crack at their weakest point" (2009, p. 21). The tetrapus' tentacles eventually lose their cohesiveness under the weakness, and the center slowly loses its stronghold over society as the fissures in its foundation open minute pathways for resistance to occur. We can apply Galtung's assertion to our hypothetical mass man as well, for the corporation personified is an embodiment of a globalized imperialist agenda. What is his weakest point? With his insatiable thirst for power, the mass man, the corporation personified by the U.S. Supreme Court, is rendered incapable of discerning *how* and *when* to stop (Galtung, 2009). And because he places no value in understanding his own history, he has no cognition that failure is even a possibility.

1858 marked the year of the East India Company's official collapse. During its 250 year reign of terror, the East India Company weathered through countless parliamentary proceedings addressing its mismanagement (but interestingly not corruption). It survived wars, famines and droughts in India, bankruptcies, and rebellions against its taxation policies. But the one area it could not survive was its hearing in the court of public opinion. The first 150 years of the East India Company enamored the British elite as they found themselves drenched in the money that was being made literally by the pounds. But as the stories of Indian suffering and exploitation at the hands of the company began to reach Britain's mainland, public opinion began to waiver. As a result, no longer a symbol of prosperity, the East India

Company came to be viewed as a symbol of shame. Indeed, for a country infatuated with its own history, any evidence of the company's existence save for an over-sized marble carving etched in a foyer wall of its former London office still erect has been virtually erased out of Britain's history books; a blemish concealed from the pages of time.

While public opinion was dissipating on the mainland, after having survived the brutal side of the imperial spectrum for 250 years, India's citizens had finally reached their limit and rebelled. When the company began requiring soldiers to use shell cartridges greased with pork or beef fat before placing them in rifles, the soldiers found this sufficient cause to mutiny against the company's army. Not that the greased cartridges were the problem, but they now had to be bitten in order to fit into the rifle, and with Hindu and Muslim doctrines prohibiting the ingestion of beef or pork, the soldiers saw the requirement as a direct violation of their religion. Their initial mutiny against the policy soon evolved into a full-scale citizen's rebellion against the entire company for the right to define freedom for themselves. Battle after bloody battle ensued, accumulating a substantial Indian death toll. But as the dust settled, India emerged victorious, Britain licked its wounds and retreated from the country, and Parliament dissolved the company shortly thereafter.

The lesson to be learned by our hypothetical mass man is that human beings capable of defining love beyond the realm of good and evil will only tolerate exploitative practices for so long before they reach a point where resistance, revolt, or revolution no longer harbors a fear *greater* than the fear of remaining silenced within a system of exploitation. In other words, they no longer have anything left to lose. There are rumblings of this resistance occurring in the U.S. in relation to the mass man's exploitative practices for the purpose of higher profits and insatiable thirsts for power.

With the mass man having blanketed the media with contemptuous or hate-filled rhetoric associated with topics ranging from healthcare to women's rights to choose, to the evils of higher education, coupled with the loss of jobs due to outsourcing, ecological destruction, oil spills contradicting the argument for more off-shore drilling, multiple wars on terror, increases in insurance premiums and costs of living while salaries are being furloughed, and the privatization of anything that will stand still long enough to label it with a for-sale sign including Medicare, Medicaid, social security and public education, many people have simply reached their limit. Add to this brutal equation mind-numbing policies emerging out of the ALEC imperial policy-mill that protects corporate interests at the expense of human needs, I believe people are waking up from their slumber of indifference and recognizing that human beings are more than externalities or collateral damages or images to avoid or erase. Many are tired of living an atomized existence and wish to reconnect as human beings were intended. And because they may have already lost their jobs or their homes or their connections to loved ones, they may have also lost their fear.

That is where we must enter the fold as teachers. We have to realize that silence will get us nowhere but further into the self-obliteration process where we revolt, but only against ourselves. We are going to have to join forces with teachers in Wisconsin and Chicago in order to let our voice be heard. And because the mass man's greatest lesson learned was how to scream the loudest, we are going to need a bullhorn. What the teachers in these two states have accomplished is to re-awaken the possibilities, re-open the empty chest and re-insert their hearts back into their lived experiences. They have demonstrated hope that a new path beyond Frost's two roads is not only possible, but plausible. And, most importantly I believe, they have exposed the limitation in the belief that corporations should have carte blanche in and over society because *they* create jobs. In so doing, these teachers-as-subjects have renewed the possibilities that we may create pathways for ourselves. Now we must capture the momentum, insert the pirate, and then act accordingly. For me, this action involves outlaw pedagogy, and it is to this pedagogy we now turn.

CHAPTER 7

WELCOME THE OUTLAW

Piracy as a Pedagogy of Possibility

LOOKING BACK, SO AS TO MOVE FORWARD

Chapters five and six presented us with a conjecture to demonstrate the degree in which corporations impress on even the most minute of details in our lives. As Bakon asserts, "Today, corporations govern our lives. They determine what we eat, what we watch, what we wear, where we work, and what we do. We are inescapably surrounded by their culture, iconography, and ideology" (2004, p. 5). What makes *Pirates of the Caribbean* so compelling is its demonstration of the degree in which the corporation will strive to sustain that power, even by reducing government to a subordinate position, as Beckett did to Governor Swann. Of course, by presenting the exploitation of power in a historical context, imperialism and colonization can be re-presented as no longer influencing contemporary culture because it supposedly died alongside the collapse of the East India Company. Even if we align our interpretation of freedom with historical pirates instead of Sparrow's, the pirate films' suggest there is nothing left to resist. This belief proves false when one compares the hidden curriculum embedded in the pirate trilogy with current exploitative practices conducted by today's trans-national corporations, with imperialism and colonization redressing in economic globalized and recolonized clothing.

Equally compelling is how *Pirates of the Caribbean* reflects Foucault's notion or power and resistance as never outside of each other but always intricately bound at multiple locations. Exploitation and abuse occur when either of the two concepts gain the upper hand and is indiscriminate of whether the imbalance occurs on an individual level or on a grand, systemic scale. In this respect, pirates serve as a cultural barometer, appearing in "weird and strange places" on the space-time continuum to inform others that grand scale structures of power have surpassed its adversary in the struggle.

Piracy reached its peak in the Golden Age when the East India Company's reign of terror on India, China, and the seas was gaining momentum. Wars, famines, territorial acquisitions, and ecological devastation were not enough to quench the company's insatiable thirst for power in relation to profit. Colonization joined forces with imperialism to construct conditions in which the colonized in India and elsewhere internalized the cultural attributes imposed by oppressive regimes until they could no longer identify themselves outside of these conditions.

Piracy resurged at the onset of the twenty-first century where today's trans-national corporations reign of terror gains momentum in popular cultural texts such as media, movies and other outlets able to desensitize viewers to that terror. Indeed, terror has become its own market. Wars in Iraq and Afghanistan, wide-spread famine in Africa, exploitation of workers in factories and sweatshops in China, India, and elsewhere, oil spills in the Gulf of Mexico, and the production of a cancerous generation in Somalia resulting from exposure to contaminants dumped off their coastline are not enough to thwart the corporation's insatiable thirst for power in relation to profit. Recolonization has joined forces with economic globalization to construct conditions in which the recolonized now located anywhere in the world internalize cultural attributes imposed by the corporate regime until we no longer identify ourselves outside of these conditions.

Because historical pirates refused to be defined by imperialism and colonization, they became the object of a delegitimization campaign. The assault came from the tip of a sword and the point of a pen. Likewise, because contemporary pirates resist being defined by globalization and recolonization, they are the target of a re-presentation campaign concealing the role trans-national corporations played in that resurgence. The attack comes, not from a sword but an assault rifle, not from a pen but from pixels. Technological advances made by the introduction of the Internet have provided an easy pathway for trans-national corporations to stay connected with factories no longer housed in the U.S. for reasons such as the avoidance of legislation relating to minimum wages and environmental protections. But these same advances have also provided an easy pathway for resisters to upload video files, blogs, and other texts challenging these conditions. Whereas in the past the public had to await correspondence from colonial possessions to arrive on the mainland by ship, today information is instantaneous, arriving as quickly as one is able to click a mouse.

In the past, the struggle between resistance and power, the pirate and the East India Company, resulted in a victory for power with pirates being eradicated and the East India Company left to operate unencumbered for another hundred years. During this time period, corporate exploitation and abuse ran amok until Parliament shut the company down in response to the uprising in India. Public opinion no longer favored corporate abuse. Extreme conditions are quelled for a time, but not before a seed is planted on both sides of the struggle. Pirates leave behind a pirate code some consider to be a prototype for democratic principles. These principles will be utilized by the masses of people relocating to the American colonies to construct a democratic government after the Revolution. The East India Company leaves us with a prototype of a trans-national corporation engaging in the trade of stock. Both sides of the power struggle influence how the U.S. will define itself in the future.

Over the course of U.S. history, power and resistance collide in multiple locations, each learning something in the exchange. Take the Civil War, for example. Slavery is abolished in the States, reconstruction is imposed on the South, and citizenry is contested in the Courts. Resistance declares victory when citizenship is broadened to include newly-freed slaves, but power undermines that victory when personhood is broadened to include the corporation. So the powerful reap the rewards of a separate but equal doctrine in that they are freed from the burden of taxation from multiple states in which they operate, and the weak get their own water fountain. A Great Depression resulting from stock market crashes, bank collapses, economic tensions affecting relations with Europe, and drought in the U.S. cripples the corporation for a while, but a world war bails them out. President Franklin Roosevelt then instills a New Deal to prevent another wide-scale collapse from occurring in the future with strict regulations placed on corporate activity to protect individual consumers. Resistance wins this round of the struggle, but not before power hires an attorney to identify and exploit the loopholes.

Other events in U.S. history include Women's Suffrage coinciding with the re-presentation of propaganda as public relations. Vietnam protests are met with Human Potential Movements where we learn to define ourselves by what we purchase rather than what we believe. The exploitation of U.S. workers is countered by unions designed to protect them. Civil Rights are countered by racism shifting from blatant to more subtle forms now masking itself behind various institutions in society. Women enter the workforce but at substantially less pay. Our male counterparts then fault us for societal ills because our absence in the kitchen has resulted in the breakdown of the family-and not just any family, but a nuclear kind, with a mother, father, 2.2 children, a dog, a cat, or both. We live in an age consisting of a war on terror, an attack on freedom, an assault on religion coupled with a war on Christmas. The 2008 election of the U.S.'s first black president was matched by total gridlock in Congress along political party lines who feign ignorance when racism is suggested as one of many causes. The Great Depression was matched by a great recession in which corporate greed resulting from Reagan's deregulation campaign shifted the balance of power back in favor of the corporation which by that time had extended its tentacles of power globally.

As a result of deregulation, media moguls such as Rupert Murdoch were able to purchase multiple media outlets including filmed entertainment, cable and television outlets, and numerous global newspaper organizations, ensuring that his message is represented as *the* message by those whose exposure to "news" is limited to one or all outlets owned by him. So when piracy resurges, the message is framed as a threat to freedom because it threatens efficient flows of money now traversing the globe. Freedom as a liberation from constraints translates into a liberation of the *corporation* from constraints; the human being is irrelevant in the pursuit of profit. And because we may only ingest one perspective, we assume it to be the only perspective– score one for the side of power. However, the difference between past and present struggles with extreme conditions of power and resistance is that today we may no longer depend on our government or democratic principles to balance the equation because trans-national corporations have reduced the government to a subordinate position of power, as Beckett did to Governor Swann. The culture of fear reaches the White House as the entire country is held hostage by the corporation's threat to outsource jobs that have already been shipped overseas.

Of course, these examples reflect the more publicized instances in U.S. history where power and resistance have collided. Every day, individuals are subjected to the tyranny of oppression as they pay for gasoline they can barely afford or when they apply for a job or even as they ask their children about their day in school. Every time we sit in a car, we subject ourselves to the exploitation of legal loopholes by members of the automotive industry who determine our life to be less valuable than the few extra dollars they earn by disregarding regulations. So it should come as no surprise to witness children in schools being reduced to a single score on a high-stakes test. The testing industry produces a job for someone and that is apparently ample reason to award the industry full access to this country's youth. With support from testing mandates included in *NCLB* and *Race to the Top*, the industry receives more options in developing standardized tests, criterion-referenced tests, benchmark and predictor tests, and the student receives little choice in taking them. Of course, this is the same government which turned a blind eye to the exploitation of children working in sweatshops years ago until child labor laws were forced upon them by those resisting these conditions.

What *is* surprising is the degree in which teachers in general are not more vocal in their protests against systemic oppressions experienced in their classrooms. Certainly, there are organizations, teacher unions, and educational lobbyists countering these oppressions just as there are entire fields of inquiry such as Curriculum Studies and Social Foundations of Education dedicated to bringing attention to these issues. And much effort has been given towards rehumanizing individuals dwelling in school settings. But the number of teachers in K-12 environments who remain unaware of these organizations or the growing body of literature challenging institutional oppressions is utterly astounding. Out of the dozen or so teachers I impromptu questioned about current events relating to education, only one was able to recognize how the 2012 teachers strike in Chicago directly related to the struggles she experiences in her classroom in Macon, Georgia. The rest faulted unions for shutting down the schools and negatively impacting students, suggesting the students were not being negatively impacted by policies implemented when the school was in session. Even less were aware of how our silence contributes to the erasure of corruption from the institution of education by placing that corruption in our laps. All were cognizant of the culture of fear accompanying neoliberal policies although they dared not describe it as such. And the majority concluded they could not do much about our current circumstances other than to "make the best" of the situation. There are a host of reasons as to why we invoke our right to remain silent, but as I listened to my friends talk, specific themes emerged in relation to resistance and power which speak directly to our struggles with being caught in between the extreme conditions of power we are experiencing today.

The first possibility relates to Nietzsche's notion of master and slave morality. Just as piracy proved not to have been eradicated, slavery also appears not to have been abolished. Certainly, the historic meaning of the term no longer exists, but as a condition of being in a state of bondage, it appears we have substituted one set of chains for another in that we have become enslaved by debt. As a result, we are more susceptible to the threats of termination we routinely hear. Thus, we are not masters of our own fate because we react to conditions constructed by others. When being constantly threatened, we are mentally beaten, eventually becoming pessimistic. Schools no longer reflect the joy they once did, and morality plummets to an all new low. In the process, we embody slave morality in that we end up defining our experiences in school by determining what is good based on that already identified as evil. In this case, what is evil is the threat and what is considered "good" are behaviors that reduce the number of threats we receive.

There are some bad policies and hidden curricula circulating in schools today. But we cannot allow these negativities to define every aspect of our day. When we do, teaching becomes a life-negating encounter for us and our students. Our perpetual state of reaction does not help our situation. Rather, it helps the neoliberal ideology and corporate logic informing our situation. And because we may not understand the politics and language invoked to sustain corporate influence in the school, we may also not understand which apparatus of power we are currently struggling. We only understand the fear, and fear is bad.

The second possibility is a lesson we learn from historical representations of the pirate. When the pirate was juxtaposed with the privateer, it provided legitimacy to the latter through the delegitimizing of the former. It also gave credence to the idea that "private" automatically equates to "better" living conditions for human beings simply because it is legal. Today, the privateer has evolved into privatization, also equating to better, not only by invoking that sense of legality but also in the idea that competition between corporations to supply a need naturally results in better choices for the consumer. But the fact that we may be enslaved by debt or are not privileged enough to live on the much discussed Wall Street or Main Street, to name but two examples of exclusion, means that we may be unable to participate in that choice. Indeed, these individuals do not even register an acknowledgement in the conversation.

Sometimes, as in the case of many pirates, the choice to live a life of passion and purpose with the possibility of reclaiming a promise of freedom involves rejecting the conditions set before us and refusing to participate in the limitations imposed on our being. I will return to this possibility shortly, but for now, I conclude the point with a question for my friends which must linger in our thoughts beyond the last pages of this text: If the privateer was granted legitimacy based on the delegitimization of pirates, then what population of people currently sitting in your classrooms are being delegitimized, ignored, erased, or stereotyped to grant legitimacy for the privatization of education? I recognize variations of this question are already being explored in fields such as Curriculum Studies or Social Foundations and in the broader contexts of culture and society in relation to race, class, gender, etc. But for the K-12 teacher still unaware this body of literature exists, it is time for these individuals to consider the question as well.

The third possibility for our silence deals with the question of loyalty and represents one of the greatest sources of tension for teachers. Are we loyal to the state or to the student? The fact that we even have to ask this question demonstrates the degree in which "corporate logic" (Apple, 1995) has infiltrated schools. Our students do not ask this question, but, as was demonstrated by the Griffin-Spalding County, Georgia School Superintendent, the district inquires. To proclaim we prioritize student needs over system needs informs the district of the difficulty we may experience when being forced to conform to systemic oppressions carefully concealed from the public eye. I do not believe being loyal to students is synonymous with being disloyal to the system. To suggest that it does reflects the narrow-mindedness needed to secure control over a teacher's actions. Yet when we are loyal to the system, we risk not seeing some of the students in our class. For the ones who do not test well and are deemed "hopeless learners" by the system, as some children were delegated by my former principal, they may not be offered any instruction by a teacher who seizes the permission granted by school administration to ignore that child in order to focus time and attention to those who "matter" to the school's bottom line, that is, to AYP; the energy and effort spent on teaching the "hopeless learner" is deemed to be a non-profitable use of time. At a period when children are being thrust behind the numbers scored on a high-stakes test, the question of loyalty matters, yet many of my friends have never given the question much thought.

Our pragmatic desire to solve a problem or resolve the tensions and anxieties we feel when caught between the pirate and the corporation personified leads to a fourth reason we may remain silent. In our desire to resolve tensions quickly, we search for the path of least resistance, claim a spot on that path, and await our anxieties to subside as we walk blindly down a road dictated by others. In so doing, we avoid a necessary struggle with potential reasons as to *why* we feel anxious. With indifference being celebrated in popular cultural spaces such as *Pirates of the Caribbean*, and an intimate bedfellow of neoliberal ideology in its desire to isolate and atomize the individual, we cease talking about our struggles in productive ways that may lead to challenges within the school and larger district. We become nihilists, as Nietzsche depicts, and revolt against ourselves, as Gasset warns. These reactions are why Davy Jones is crucial to education because he symbolizes what can happen to us, not when we become corrupt (for are we not already in that state when we accept uncontested corrupt interpretations of learning?) but when we become indifferent to the Other and ignore our social responsibility for the betterment of all.

Antonia Darder describes these tensions in her comparison between traditional methods of teaching and progressive methods associated with more revolutionary pedagogies. For Darder, the degree of tension is predominantly determined by the degree in which local or district-level school systems align themselves to both formal and informal systems of power. Whereas more traditional approaches tend to reinforce dominating beliefs and practices in culture and society in relation to race, class, gender, sexuality, etc. while operating to objectify the teacher and student, Darder argues revolutionary pedagogies reinsert the subjectivity involved within discursive practices, allowing for teachers and students to learn together, through and with each other as questions relating to power structures how knowledge is constructed in relation to these structures are reflected. Reflection leads to more thoughtful questions leading to a better understanding of how we arrived at our current location as well as the role culture plays in helping us reach that point. Darder calls the experiences of tension natural experiences when we practice "teaching against the grain" (2002, p. 134). The teacher-pirate engages the tension and does not run from it. She constantly questions and reflects on her actions to determine where her loyalties lie in each situation. Because she does not view the world in terms of good/ evil, she does not dwell on questions of disloyalty because she understands a loyalty to students does not work against a system which claims that "Our students are why we are here" (2012, Website) but offers challenges to those beliefs and behaviors undermining that claim.

It is important to note that pirates did not reject authority or else they would never have consented to the pirate code. The code placed limitations on their actions but the limitations were designed to ensure an optimal degree of freedom to all who boarded. What pirates rejected was the authoritarianism experienced whiles on land via class oppressions or on board merchant vessels via captain predation, both of which were granted legitimacy by the same system relegating their place as the piratical Other.

Darder distinguishes between the two modes of power by telling us,

Authority refers to the power teachers possess to influence (direct) learning, thought, and behavior through their responsibility to educate students; authoritarianism is linked to the expectation that students should and will blindly accept and submit to the concentration of power in the hands of the teacher as the exclusive knowing subject. (2002, p. 113)

We can expound on Darder's distinction to include the power corporations now possess in influencing the construction of policies now inundated in the school experience. The expectation is that teachers blindly accept these conditions without challenging them lest they be terminated. Authority seeks to affirm life as it discusses which elements may be good and which may be bad. Authoritarianism seeks to negate life as discussion is annihilated because anything evil has already been designated as that which undermines its power. And part of the tension we experience in relation to loyalty is that by prioritizing student needs over system needs, we undermine the system's power it wields over our immediate actions.

The final reason is a culmination of the previous concerns in that as we question, reflect, and understand the gravity of our situation, we begin to feel as if any challenge we may offer will be futile, so we accept current conditions in defeat. In our acceptance, we come to see ourselves the way authoritarian regimes of power view us, through our failures rather than our successes, in contempt. This is where I believe we may learn the most from pirates, countering our feelings by building confidence in our actions. Peter Wilson once suggested pirates should be studied "as a form of social resistance" (1995, p. 22); the key word being resistance. As teachers, it is difficult to behave as historical pirates and reject the entire system of education because our connection to classroom spaces is what breathes life into our existence. But there are elements of the pirate that teach us how to resist our oppressions in ways that lead to reclaiming classroom spaces for ourselves and our students and against the corporate logic in schools seeking to narrow our interpretation of freedom by making us indifferent to other perspectives. These elements inform outlaw pedagogy, and it is to this pedagogy we make our final turn.

CHARTING A COURSE THROUGH OUTLAW PEDAGOGY

One may find it peculiar to conclude a text with the introduction of a pedagogical encounter. In ordinary circumstances, I might agree. But these are no ordinary circumstances. The reappearance of the pirate at this location in history informs us thusly. This text has served as a historiography of how I arrived at my current locale, as a teacher struggling with extreme conditions of imbalance between power and resistance. Questions I now consider seek to keep these tensions at the forefront of my thoughts. How do I navigate through the uncertainty being "in-between" provokes in such a way that limits my limitations while not avoiding them? How do I work inside a system of education without falling prey to the indifference that system requires when dehumanizing my existence, diminishing my enthusiasm, and destroying my passion?

We may navigate the vast terrain this question affords by first discerning and then articulating boisterously where our loyalties reside- with people. For if our loyalties are not with people, we are not working against current systems of imperial oppressions dominating contemporary school discourse, we are perpetuating them. As stated in the previous chapter, this loyalty does not operate outside of the conditions of one's contract. On the contrary, it brings to mind who we are working for and with, and what we are working against. Outlaw pedagogy does not ask us to work outside the law. Rather, it requires a dedication to work outside the cultural norms and assumptions constructing the conditions in which laws are perceived and then written. Only by focusing on our humanity and the promise an education affords may our humanity and that promise be restored.

Second, inquiry into how we may approach classroom conversations which continuously promote a mutual exchange of ideas must be made. Outlaw pedagogy blends together elements of critical and deconstructive pedagogies with a set of loose conditions Gabriel Kuhn used to identify the pirate as a condition on which classroom conversations may be analyzed to ensure its dialogical openness. By coupling these pedagogies with the piratical passion needed to pursue a promise of freedom outside of a neoliberal narrowing of the term, freedom reappears on the horizon and our classrooms become the ships we board to pursue life's possibilities.

Finally, we may thwart indifference by responding to Darder's call to re-invent Freire in the context of individual lived experiences. This is a crucial element to Outlaw pedagogy because what may be blatantly outlawed in one school may be quietly accepted in another. Yet always a question to consider in any situation is the degree in which school structures and cultural hegemony perpetuate themselves within the environment through others and our own reactions. Freire teaches, "The progressive educator must always be moving out on his or her own, continually reinventing me and reinventing what it means to be democratic in his or her own specific cultural and historical context" (in Darder, 2002, vi). To accept Freire's words at face-value would render a disservice to his work, ignoring critical pedagogy's intentions rather than bestowing honor. Oh sure, we may now claim to teach from a Freirian perspective, asking more questions but not necessarily more thoughtful questions, but our acceptance would be mere substitution if our questions were also not directed inward at our habits and how they inform our thoughts and experiences.

Thus, outlaw pedagogy begins with Freire's call to inquiry. We ask questions. Initially, whether our questions are considered "good" or "bad" is irrelevant. What matters is that we ask; as Freire and Faundez attest, "learning to question" (1989) is a process, an embarkation into the unknown with no preconceived ideas of where we might emerge. Learning to voice concern amidst growing hostility in the workplace will have to be a public struggle, moving from quiet conversations with colleagues to vocalizing concerns in department meetings, then faculty meetings, and hopefully moving outwards to include district-level and eventually larger systemic oppressions on the federal and global level.

By asking questions, the catachresis reveals itself and our inquiries forge a path into the realm of deconstruction. What would Spivak ask at this juncture? I believe she would ask us to consider how we might work inside the boundaries of imperial codifications embedded in systems of language while simultaneously challenging them, always moving outwards into the peripheries rather than being blindly engulfed by some violent imperial center. Lather would follow suit by asking us to consider how our challenges inadvertently support the systems of oppression and boundaries we advocate against.

These two questions, when taken together, reflect the recursivity underlining outlaw pedagogy. It is what William Doll depicts as looping, telling us, "Such looping, thoughts on thoughts, distinguishes human consciousness; it is the way we make meaning" (1993, p. 177). For Doll, meaning-making experiences no beginning or end and reveals itself in dialogical encounters with others. We tend to the dialogue, nurturing the process as we monitor the conversation to ensure and sustain its openness. We pose questions such as, what are the external factors shaping the words we use to describe a particular experience? How do these same factors operate to define the conditions of a choice to be made stemming from the experience? Our definition is where we may identify catachrestic boundaries. Through our questions the boundaries previously concealed behind our words slowly emerge into view, subsequently informing how we interpret and analyze the systems of power in which we live and interact.

As we learn to question differently, we learn to read our experiences differently, and the possibility of acting against our oppressions takes on new and distinct forms which then must be questioned, reflected upon, acted upon, looping together as thoughts create new thoughts, questions create new questions, reflections create new reflections; a perpetual state of creation leads to a kinetic state of becoming master of our own fate-always moving. Doll is careful to distinguish recursion from repetition by reminding us of the need for *conscious* exploration, dialogue, and constructive criticism as we reflect on the language used in articulating the exploratory process. "Dialogue," he argues, "becomes the sine qua non of recursion: without reflection-engendered by dialogue- recursion becomes shallow not transformative; it is not reflective recursion, it is only repetition" (1993, p. 178). Repetition works to close the conversation. Repetition is what traditional practices of teaching perpetuate-the old drill and kill method. Repetition deadens dialogue in its dictation of the conditions in which conversations may occur. Am I repeating myself?

Recursion works in the opposite direction, working to open dialogue, granting us the space needed to question encounters of entrapment such as when we sign our contract to discern the hidden conditions of our employment. Recursion is how dialogue traverses critical and deconstructive pedagogies, connects Freire's work with Doll's, my work with pirates, all of our work with each other's. Recursion as a perpetual state of creation, thoughts on thoughts, building, deconstructing, moving inside or out, to the left or to the right, emulates Kuhn's identification of pirates as molecular beings. Pirates were a "fluctuating pack," Kuhn informs, "constantly in motion, changing in number or composition from one month to the next" (1997, p. 229). Sometimes they boarded a ship at one port only to arrive at a new location on a completely different vessel. Egalitarian communities were short-lived, but the ethos connecting one pirate ship to another was always present. This mobility is a necessary condition of curriculum if it is to flourish; sometimes this idea, sometimes that, sometimes direct instruction, sometimes cooperative learning, always listening, with a recursive, kinetically energized and dialogical ethos connecting one experience to another. As teachers, we, too, engage in mobility, sometimes on this committee, sometimes on that, sometimes teaching one grade level only to teach another next year; sometimes focusing on mathematical concepts only to move into language after lunch; always moving.

The difference between the pirate and teachers is that becoming molecular, as Kuhn argues, was a fundamental condition of piracy, not just in relation to mobility but also in equality. There were no distinctions between crew-members granting authority of one over any other save for the captain, and he could be replaced at a moment's notice. According to the pirate code, three or more votes in favor of ousting the captain from command could occur at any time, so the captain constantly surveyed his actions to ensure no impingement on individual interpretations of freedom occurred. He did this while also ensuring the crew could pull together as one cohesive body of force against an attack or for an opportunity to plunder at a moment's notice. For this reason, strict penalties against crew members caught unprepared for battle were included in the code, not as a negation of individual liberties, but to ensure solidarity so that freedom remained accessible to all.

As teachers, our mobility does not always lend itself to the molecularity Kuhn depicts. Grade-level or department-level meetings are now spent disaggregating data in order to label children and predict future performances on a high-stakes test. Time better spent engaging in meaningful dialogue with colleagues regarding our curricular encounters with students has been replaced with completely unnecessary and endless forms. My former principal loved meetings. He would meet to discuss upcoming meetings. I believe he just liked to hear himself talk. But every Thursday morning, our time together as a grade level would be spent completing a four-page document *about* a student as opposed to discussing the myriad ways in which we might work *with* the student to enhance learning. The principal never said a word, just watched-the realities of NCLB and *Race to the Top*. If there was any solidarity between colleagues, it was in the collective belief that the dictation of how our meeting times were to be spent resulted in our meetings always being a complete waste of time, producing a document for the police to review. Everything in a corporate-driven school environment must have a document to be entered as evidence.

In retrospect, I have come to understand these encounters as a way to split us apart, atomize each individual as we each retreated to our classroom, moving quickly to shut our doors. We were behaving exactly as was intended, and because we posed no questions, even to each other, we offered no challenge. We accepted. We were incognizant of our individual power to resist. Freire informs us of the consequences of acceptance. He states:

> I reject the notion that nothing can be done about the consequences of economic globalization and refuse to bow my head gently because nothing can be done against the unavoidable. Accepting the inexorability of what takes place is an excellent contribution to the dominant forces in their unequal fight against the 'condemned of the earth'. (1997, p, 43)

WHEN WE ACCEPT, WE CAPITULATE

The irony of Freire's statement when taken in the context of the aforementioned experience is that his words exhibit actions each one of us is capable of executing, and replicate the actions engaged by pirates: Freire rejects, and he refuses. Like the pirate, Freire rejects an idea that nothing can be done about our current circumstances. I cannot speak for pirates, but for me, understanding that I do not have to accept the conditions impressing on the school experience is both empowering and liberating. When systemic oppressions overwhelm me, I gain confidence in the knowledge that rejection is an action well within my power and my reach. Thus, rejection of the idea that nothing can be done about our current circumstances is also a necessary condition of outlaw pedagogy. It is the belief that unites our efforts as we move in infinite directions amidst the catachresis-mobile, equal, together, molecular.

What do I reject? I reject the idea that nothing can be done about the corporate influence in schools. It is not that I believe corporations are inherently bad, but because their participation in the quest for a socially-just world is inhibited by a law binding them to the pursuit of profit; there is only so much they may contribute to the human condition before impinging on profitable margins of return. And their presence in schools has participated in the dehumanization of students by mutating them into objectified test scores and teachers as robots mindlessly disaggregating their existence. Instead of shareholders investing in companies, parents and community-members are reduced to distant stakeholders investing in a test. We receive quarterly reports via semester averages, and dividends are now linked to the number of students proficient on the state-mandated test; the higher the number of students passing, the higher the dividends to the community, with the entire process stripping the humanity away from each child with each subsequent question.

I also reject the idea that nothing can be done about the erasure of corruption from the institution of education by placing that corruption in the hands of teachers. As a mode of authoritarianism, erasure severs dialogue through its narrow pursuit of blame. With no dialogue, there are no possibilities to question or to reflect with others; there is no recursivity, no kinetic energy, thus no action-the promise of freedom concealing itself behind our silence. I reject this mode of existence.

Of course, rejection provides only short-term successes. Once we reject we must explore how our rejections evolve into subsequent actions. Freire tells us exactly how his rejection evolved into subsequent action. Once he ascertained what he was rejecting, he refused. Freire refused *to ignore* the conditions of oppression imposed on others in his refusal to "bow his head." Merely tolerating our circumstances equates to ignoring the conditions of oppression. By "making the best" of circumstances, we limit our ability to make them better.

Freire also refused *to accept* the conditions of the impoverished and indignation of the privileged. Remember, to accept is to contribute, and I refuse to contribute to the idea that some children are deemed as "unprofitable" so that more time may be spent on the "able-minded," an expense paid by the child deemed "hopeless learner." Lastly, Freire refused *to believe* the conditions should cohabitate peacefully so that one population of people may continue to flourish at the expense of another who flounders. By focusing on those tasks within his reach, Freire is then able to question how the oppressions experienced, witnessed, and now understands more intimately extend beyond school boundaries, feeding into the community, the nation, the world. Yet because we also now understand our capacity to reject and refuse, what was once an overwhelming encounter becomes a new purpose, a passionate pursuit of a promise of freedom now extending beyond our own skin as we reach outside cultural boundaries to share that promise with others; always moving, always recursive, because there are always new experiences-*pirao*. That is what defines outlaw pedagogy.

IF A PIRATE I MUST BE

The molecularity of the pirate is not the only distinguishing feature teachers may observe and learn. Pirates also require space. Kuhn defines space as openings where we are free to move unobserved, and warns of a pirate's fate when space is no longer available: "If all space is carved up, then piracy is finished. Indetectability, like molecularity, is inseparable from piracy" (1997, p. 232). In the past, pirates required large spaces to conceal an entire crew and ship. The sea offered that space. But today's pirate is not burdened with this need. For the pirates of Somalia, large ships have evolved into smaller outriggers. The indetectability remains, but it is now associated with the speed at which the outrigger can approach a barge or sovereign vessel without being detected. But how does the teacher-pirate maneuver the educational terrain undetected when both our speed and our space is being impeded?

After the demise of historical pirates, technology advanced to the point where few places in which to hide remain save for the remotest of locations. But that does not also mean we cannot maneuver undetected. Today's pirate hides in plain sight, right in front of us, only visible when the mind consciously seeks and then fixates on the image for study. Today's indetectability may be likened to the words we use to describe our freedoms, and how these same words, imperially encoded before they are normalized in our lexicon, simultaneously limit our freedoms through our articulation. This was exemplified in chapter one through the normalization of pirate as strict interpretations of robber, thief, cutthroat. Another example is how we read a text to ascertain its meaning only to revisit the text months later and discover new meanings. This new meaning was hidden at first glance but was always there, waiting to be discovered upon a more thorough review. Indetectability is how social forces such as hegemony or structural violence operate in culture and society in front, around, and within us to sustain our social location. To the indifferent eye, there is nothing there to see.

On a recent trip to Boston, I observed a pirate undetected. A homeless man had pirated some public space against a building. He sat on the cold concrete, just him, his guitar, and his dog. Having traveled the subway to the Harvard/Cambridge station, I emerged from the tunnels into the intellectual nexus of the universe when the man caught my attention. Having pirated my own space a short distance from his, I watched. As people walked by, the man would yell "Don't look at me!" Repeatedly he shouted these words. Repeatedly individuals passed him by without a glance. With all of the intelligent people trespassing on that location, the homeless man proved to be the wisest of them all, for in his shouts for others *not* to notice, he was drawing attention to the fact that they already did not. "Don't look at me!" became a plea to pay attention to what is directly in front of our eyes, as he was to his trespassers. I left that location having learned more about our culture and society in the thirty minutes I observed his actions than I had studied in my entire life.

Our culture has become so conditioned to look down, at our cell phones to retrieve the latest text or email, we seem to have lost our capacity to look ahead and catch sight of that which stares us in the face. The corporation's influence in schools have capitalized on our lack of vision and constructed conditions for teachers to stand in front of their rooms and never really *see* the students for who and what they are, as people, *children*, and not some objectified image of the cold and unfeeling statistic.

Outlaw pedagogy rejects this objectification and begins to teach a curriculum designed for the living. We may teach the prescribed standard, but we do so in ways that tap into the lived experiences of the child, drawing on cultural images made popular today. And we hide in plain sight, right in front of the administrative police who scan our classrooms daily, but only catch sight of the appearance that all have conformed; the standards strategically located on the board, essential questions written atop her lesson; that is all the police demand to see.

Michael Apple once stated teachers reclaim their autonomy when they close the doors of their classroom (1995), but in today's culture of testing and fear, the teacher-pirate recognizes closed doors signal a red flag, inviting interlopers to invade the space she has created with her students. The teacher-pirate now opens her door to reclaim her autonomy. In her action, she rejects the idea that good teaching must be conducted in secret and refuses to react in fear. She is aware protests are public events and demonstrates through dialogue with her class, both reclaiming their humanity in the conversations.

The recursivity underlying outlaw pedagogy necessitates constant motion in infinite numbers and directions. Because we question, reflect, act, question again, the space, like the pirate, becomes malleable, always changing, so as to transform that space when the need arises. This is because indetectability is never a guarantee that one day we may not actually be seen. Like Richard Meyer having abandoned the punk style created once it was commodified, we will eventually be forced to abandon those activities proving successful today, with dialogue being one of many common threads weaving throughout each experience. In schools where corporate logic is always alert to change, new spaces, once visible, are commodified by normalizing the conditions that once made the space unique, draining the life out of the space until there is nothing left. This is what Disney is doing with the idea of piracy. By equating it to a business model, Disney limits new spaces potentially challenging its empire because their resisters often resist the association. So when pirates are re-presented as "good people," they are only good when taken in the context of the business model. Everyone else embracing the term equates to a corrupt and mutated Davy Jones. Yet by making the claim, then Co-Chair Ann Sweeney also reveals a weakness in her thought-the perception of piracy as stagnant. Pirates are never idle but kinetic, always moving, thinking, doing, and actively engaging in the world. Thus, activity is another property of the pirate. Kuhn describes activity in the Nietzschean sense in that pirates acted with passion and purpose on the world so as to become a part of that world. If they did not remain active, they risked having to react to an assault unprepared. The image of the stagnant pirate reflects death, not life; a hopeful indication that piracy as a business model will experience a short life.

Outlaw pedagogues are always alert to the conditions around us. We listen, look, learn, always moving into uncharted waters with our students. To stay active is to stay alive, drawing on individual wills to power evolving in the classroom. We do not react to new demands made by the administrative police because we reject the pressures of testing and fear and refuse to allow them to define us. Throughout this process, our confidence builds, our will to power strengthens and the possibility of greater challenges to larger systemic oppressions are perceived; the promise of freedom appears brighter. Laws are not written in blood. They, too, are malleable and can be changed. Thus, structures of power must impress on the individual so as to quell a desire for him to *want* laws to change. This is precisely why we must work outside cultural norms; if what is considered "normal" shifts, changes to laws sometimes evolve emulating that shift.

The third element Kuhn argues identifies the pirate is responsibility. "What is piratical order?" he asks, "Individual responsibility instead of statist-societal expectations: responsibility instead of duty" (p. 238). Responsibility is why loyalty is not *a* question asked by pirates, it is *the* question; without loyalty, molecularity in the sense of solidarity cannot occur. When teachers are loyal to students, always changing from one year or semester to another, then activity tends to flow in the direction of the students and not the state. Our efforts become a responsibility we have with students instead of a duty imposed on students for the benefit of the state.

Derrida argues when claiming to be responsible one must always question to what or to whom we are responding because in our response to one thing, something else is neglected in the process (1995). Thus, if our response is to our duty, then we do so at the expense of the students we are employed to teach. As Spalding County Schools suggest, "Our students are why we are here" (2012, Website). But if our response is to students, to educate and learn together as we share the lived experience we call curriculum, then our students are not being neglected. Our duties may be neglected (perhaps we arrive late for a meeting), but only because we are addressing a student need. And responding to students' needs is a far greater responsibility than merely attending to the needs of the State. We can do the latter when consciously attending to the former. For when we do, the challenges needed to be made inside each school and system will be vocalized out of that responsibility.

The last element Kuhn associates with pirate life discusses death. For pirates, life was about quality. This belief stemmed from the "determination to 'really live, or die trying'" (p. 244). They were aware their life-span diminished greatly when boarding a pirate ship, but the benefits far outweighed the risks. It is like the question Davy Jones posed to all his victims save Mercer: die now, or later. For pirates, life's choices posed a similar threat, die sooner as a result of pirating (after all, pirating was, and still is, a dangerous path) or die later; a slow, painful death at the hands of captain predation or class oppressions causing poverty, starvation, disease and social dis-ease. Our pain stems from recognizing how we never seized the opportunity to explore what it meant to *really live*, from accepting these conditions thus contributing to them, and then having to live with the regret acceptance often brings.

This empty existence represented a far greater fear than an immediate death at the hand of a sword or a hanging. And piracy afforded them the opportunity to explore what it meant to live a life of meaning always in the pursuit of freedom. "The pirate wants to live to the full, intensely...or not at all" (Kuhn, 1997, p. 244). And because of the other elements, molecularity, indetectability, activity, space, responsibility, solidarity, equality, with the promise of freedom revealing itself through each of these elements, pirates lived an existence worth dying for.

As teachers, we are not exposed to the same level of violence as pirates, but the question of death is one I believe we must ask. So I pose one final question for you to consider, reflect, and possibly act: At a time when we are being mentally beaten by the corporate logic inundating public schools, when morality has plummeted to an all new low and our spirit, enthusiasm, and passions may already be experiencing decay, then are we not dying already? And if we are going to die, then does it not seem pertinent to seize the few moments we have left and really *live them*? My greatest fear is that when I reach the point in life when I am no longer self-sufficient and too old and too tired to make a difference in this world, I do not want to glance backwards at my years and regret what could have been if I had only had the courage to act. No, I want to look backwards, understanding that my life was worth living, and I lived it.

Bartholomew Roberts did not enter piracy by choice. He was captured by Captain Howel Davis while on board a merchant vessel. But as he observed the crew, witnessing the camaraderie, the equality shared, the freedom they appeared to possess, and the joy reflected on their faces, his initial disdain for his captors soon gave way to respect. Four months later, when Davis was killed in an attack, Roberts was voted as Captain. He loudly proclaimed one of the most cited statements in pirate sub-culture: "I have dipped my hands in muddy water, and if a pirate I must be, 'tis better being a commander than a common man" (in Sanders, 2007, p. 57). For Roberts, the common man was he who accepted the conditions set forth by others blindly, what Nietzsche and Gasset would later call the masses. And since he had already made the mental transition to pirate life, he may as well embrace it completely, with the passion and purpose befitting the pirate he now was.

Outlaw Pedagogy requires the same level of commitment, to teach with the passion and purpose necessary if we are to reclaim classroom spaces with our students. So I conclude my text by pirating Robert's words. I do not think he will object (nor Sanders neither, who records the words I now steal): If a teacher-pirate I must be, 'tis better to be in command of my own space and master of my own fate than to be a common person who accepts, contributes, and subsequently decays under the pressures to conform, for if I choose the latter, I may as well already be dead.

I am a teacher, not a technician. I do more than take attendance. And I saw the smirk on the hypothetical mass man's face as I left the movie theatre, but his arrogance blinded his view of mine. His strength is also his weakness - the insatiable thirst for control. Yet one cannot control the hope of another. Thus, the smile I wear is a pirate smile, for I know now where I stand – as an Outlaw. I stand inside the boundaries marked by the promise and peril of the lived experience - *pirao*.

REFERENCES

Abdi, A. (1998, November 1). Education in Somalia: History, destruction, and calls for reconstruction. *Comparative Education, 34*(3), 327–340.

Adams, J. (1773). *The Boston tea party* (Digital Document # GLC 1787). Retrieved October 9, 2011, from http://www.digitalhistory.uh.edu/documents/documents_p2.cfm?doc=252

Ahmed, A. J. (1995). Preface. In A. J. Ahmed (Ed.), *The invention of Somalia* (pp. 9–15). Trenton, NJ: The Red Sea Press.

Ali, A. H. (2010). *Nomad: From Islam to America: A personal journey through the clash of civilizations.* New York, NY: Free Press.

Apple, M. W. (1995). *Education and power* (2nd ed.). New York, NY: Routledge.

Asher, N. (2009). Decolonization and education: Locating pedagogy and self at the interstices in global times. In R. S. Coloma (Ed.), *Postcolonial challenges in education* (pp. 67–77). New York, NY: Peter Lang.

Atkinson, E. (2002, March 1). The responsible anarchist: Postmodernism and social change. *British Journal of Sociology of Education, 23*(1), 73–87.

Axe, D. (2009). 10 things you didn't know about Somali pirates. *Current,* 31–33.

Ayers, W. (2004). *Teaching towards freedom: Moral commitment and ethical action in the classroom.* Boston, MA: Beacon Press.

Bahadur, J. (2011). *The pirates of Somalia: Inside their hidden world.* New York, NY: Pantheon Books.

Bakon, J. (2004). *The corporation: The pathological pursuit of profit and power.* Ontario, CN: The Penguin Group.

Baring-Gould, S. (1908). *Devonshire characters and strange events.* London, UK: John Lane (Electronic Book). Retrieved October 12, 2011, from http://books.google.com/ebooks/reader?id=c90MAAAAY AAJ&printsec=frontcover&output=reader

Barnes, V. L., & Boddy, J. (1994). *Aman: The story of a Somali girl.* New York, NY: Vintage Books.

Bedi, B., & Sehi, D. (Producers). (2005, August 1). *Mangal Pandey: the rising.* (DVD).

Bolster, W. J. (1997). *Black jacks: African American seamen in the age of sail.* Cambridge, MA: Harvard University Press.

Bowen, K. (2012, March 3). *Attacking the ivory tower* (Website) (para. 1). Retrieved June 9, 2012, from http://bpr.berkeley.edu/2012/03/attacking-the-ivory-tower/

Bowers, M. J., Wilson, R. E., & Hyde, R. L. (2011, June 30). (Special Report to Governor of Georgia). Retrieved December 10, 2011, from http://www.ajc.com/news/volume-1-of-special-1000798.html

Bruckheimer, J. (Producer). (2003). *Pirates of the Caribbean: The curse of the black pearl* [DVD]. Burbank, CA: Walt Disney Pictures.

Bruckheimer, J. (Producer). (2006). *Pirates of the Caribbean: Dead man's chest* [DVD]. Burbank, CA: Walt Disney Pictures.

Bruckheimer, J. (Producer). (2007). *Pirates of the Caribbean: At world's end* [DVD]. Burbank, CA: Walt Disney Pictures.

Bush, G. W. (2001, May 21). *Commencement address at Yale University.* New Haven, CT. (Website). Retrieved June 18, 2012, from http://www.presidency.ucsb.edu/ws/index.php?pid=45895

Bush, G. W. (2009, January 21). *President George w. Bush message to the American legislative exchange council* (Video File). Retrieved September 7, 2012, from http://www.youtube.com/watch?v=UwAgjB1IEF0

Carr, P. R. (2011). *Does your vote count: Critical pedagogy and democracy.* New York, NY: Peter Lang.

Chomsky, N. (2007). *What we say goes: Conversations on U.S. power in a changing world.* New York, NY: Metropolitan Books.

Cole, M., & Hill, D. (1995). Games of despair and rhetorics of resistance: Postmodernism, education and reaction. *British Journal of Sociology of Education, 16*(2), 165–182.

Cole, M., Hill, D., & Rikowski, G. (1997). Between postmodernism and nowhere: The predicament of the postmodern. *British Journal of Sociology of Education, 45*(2), 187–200.

REFERENCES

Colleluori, S., & Powell, C. (2012, May 9). *How ALEC is quietly influencing education reform in Georgia* (Website). Retrieved September 4, 2012, from Media Matters for America: http://mediamatters.org/research/2012/05/09/how-alec-is-quietly-influencing-education-refor/184156

Coloma, R. S., Means, A., & Kim, A. (2009). Palimpsest histories and catachrestic interventions. In R. S. Coloma (Ed.), *Postcolonial challenges in education* (pp. 3–22). New York, NY: Peter Lang.

Cordingly, D. (1996). *Under the black flag: The romance and the reality of life among the pirates.* New York, NY: Random House.

Crispin, A. C. (2011). *The price of freedom.* New York, NY: Disney Enterprises.

Curran, B. (2007). *Lost lands, forgotten realms.* Pompton Plains, NJ: Career Press, Inc.

Darder, A. (2002). *Reinventing Paulo freire: A pedagogy of love.* Cambridge, MA: Westview Press.

De Rugy, V. (2009, July 1). *Paying the pirate's price* (Online Periodical). Retrieved November 18, 2011, from http://reason.com/archives/2009/06/15/paying-the-pirates-price

Defoe, D. (1999[1972]). *A general history of the pyrates.* In M. Schonhorn (Ed.). Mineola, NY: Dover Publications.

Derrida, J. (1974). *Of grammatology.* In G. C. Spivak (Trans.). Baltimore, MD: The Johns Hopkins University Press.

Derrida, J. (1981). *Dissemination.* In B. Johnson (Trans.). Chicago, IL: University of Chicago Press.

Derrida, J. (1995). *The gift of death and literature in secret.* In D. Wills (Trans.). Chicago, IL: University of Chicago Press.

Dirks, N. B. (2006). *The scandal of empire: India and the creation of imperial Britain.* Cambridge, MA: The Belknap Press of Harvard University Press.

Doll, W. E. (1993). *A post-modern perspective on curriculum.* New York, NY: Teachers College Press.

Education, U. S. D. O. (2009, November 1). *Race to the top executive summary.* Retrieved December 10, 2011, from http://www2.ed.gov/programs/racetothetop/executive-summary.pdf

Eichstaedt, P. (2010). *Pirate state: Inside Somalia's terrorism at sea.* Chicago, IL: Lawrence Hill Books.

Fairtest.org. (2011). *Tests, cheating and educational corruption* (Website). Retrieved December 12, 2011, from http://www.fairtest.org/sites/default/files/Cheating_Fact_Sheet_8-17-11.pdf

Fanon, F. (1963). *The wretched of the earth.* New York, NY: Grove Press.

Fiske, J. (1989). *Reading the popular.* New York, NY and London, UK: Routledge.

Foucault, M. (1977). *Discipline & punish: The birth of a prison.* In A. Sheridan (Trans.). New York, NY: Random House.

Foucault, M. (1978). *The history of sexuality: An introduction volume I.* In R. Hurley (Trans.). New York, NY: Vintage Books.

Freire, P. (1970). *Pedagogy of the oppressed.* New York, NY: Continuum.

Freire, P. (1997). *Pedagogy of the heart.* New York, NY and London, UK: Continuum.

Freire, P. (2007). *Daring to dream: Toward a pedagogy of the unfinished.* Boulder, CO: Paradigm.

Freire, P., & Faundez, A. (1989). *Learning to question: A pedagogy of liberation.* Geneva, Switzerland: WCC Publications.

Fromm, E. (1976). *To have or to be?* New York, NY: Continuum.

Frost, R. (2008[1874]). *Poetry for young people: Robert Frost.* In G. D. Schmidt (Ed.). New York, NY and London, UK: Sterling.

Gallini, C. (1996). Mass exoticisms. In I. Chambers & L. Curti (Eds.), *The post-colonial question: Common skies/divided horizons* (pp. 212–220). London, UK and New York, NY: Routledge.

Galtung, J. (1996). *Peace by peaceful means: Peace and conflict, development and civilization.* London, UK: Sage.

Galtung, J. (2009). *The fall of the U.S. empire- and then what? successors, regionalization or globalization? U.S. fascism or U.S. blossoming?.* Switzerland: Transcend University Press.

Georgia, S. O. (2006). *Contract of agreement for educators.*

Giroux, H. A. (2011). *Zombie politics and culture in the age of capitalism.* New York, NY: Peter Lang.

Giroux, H. A., & Pollock, G. (2010). *The mouse that roared: Disney and the end of innocence.* Lanham, MD: Rowman & Littleford.

Giroux, H. A., & Simon, R. I. (1989). Popular culture as a pedagogy of pleasure and meaning. In H. A. Giroux, R. I. Simon & Contributors (Eds.), *Popular culture: Schooling & everyday life* (pp. 1–29). New York, NY: Bergin & Garvey.

Gosse, P. (1988[1932]). *The history of piracy.* New York, NY: Tudor Publishing.

Greene, M. (1988). *The dialectic of freedom.* New York, NY and London, UK: Teachers College Press.

Griffin-Spalding County School District. (2012). (Website). Retrieved June 26, 2012, from http://www.spalding.k12.ga.us/education/district/district.php?sectiondetailid=1&

Grossberg, L. (1989). Pedagogy in the present: Politics, postmodernity, and the popular. In H. A. Giroux, R. I. Simon & Contributors (Eds.), *Popular culture: Schooling & everyday life* (pp. 91–115). New York, NY: Bergin & Garvey.

Habib, I. (2006). Introduction: Marx's perception of India. In I. Husain, I. Habib & P. Patnaik (Eds.), *Karl Marx on India* (pp. 19–54). New Delhi, India: Tulika Books.

Hall, S. (1996). When was the post-colonial? Thinking at the limit. In I. Chambers & L. Curti (Eds.), *The post-colonial question: Common skies/divided horizons* (pp. 242–260). London and New York: Routledge.

Heidegger, M. (1971). *On the way to language.* New York: HarperCollins.

Herman, E. S., & Chomsky, N. (1988). *Manufacturing consent: The political economy of the mass media.* New York, NY: Vintage Books.

Hooks, B. (2000). *All about love: New visions.* New York, NY: Harper Perennial.

Interview with Abdulrashid Muse Mohammad (2009, June 15). Video File. Retrieved October 30, 2011, from http://www.youtube.com/watch?v=_jVUP33n0Js

Jones, C. L. (2012). Be encouraged. In *The GSCS Communicator* (Website). Retrieved June 26, 2012, from http://archive.constantcontact.com/fs018/1102609498526/archive/1109809538416.html

Kincheloe, J. L. (2010). *Knowledge and critical pedagogy: Explorations of educational purpose.* New York, NY: Springer.

Klein, N. (2007). *The shock doctrine: The rise of disaster capitalism.* New York, NY: Picador.

K'Naan. (2009, April 12). *Why we don't condemn our pirates* (Website). Retrieved November 3, 2011, from The Huffington Post http://www.huffingtonpost.com/michael-vazquez/on-pirates_b_186015.html

Konstam, A. (2006). *Blackbeard: America's most notorious pirate.* Hoboken, NJ: John Wiley & Sons.

Kuhn, G. (1997). Life under the death's head: Anarchism and piracy. In U. Klausmann, M. Meinzerin & G. Kuhn (Eds.), *Women pirates and the politics of the jolly roger* (pp. 227–280). London, UK and New York, NY: Black Rose Books.

Kuhn, G. (2010). *Life under the jolly roger: Reflections on golden age piracy.* Oakland, CA: PM Press.

Lather, P. (1991). *Getting smart: Feminist research and pedagogy with/in the postmodern.* New York, NY and London, UK: Routledge.

Leeson, P. T. (2009). *The invisible hook: The hidden economics of pirates.* Princeton, NJ: Princeton University Press.

Lewis, B. R. (2008). *The pirate code: From honorable thieves to modern-day villains.* Guilford, CT: The Lyon's Press.

Limbaugh, R. (2012, February 29). *Video File.* Retrieved June 8, 2012, from http://www.youtube.com/watch?v=6wa5wRJPG84

Lugosi, C. (2006). If I were a corporation, I'd be a constitutional person, too. *Texas Review of Law and Politics, 10,* 427–447. Retrieved March 10, 2011, from http://www.trolp.org/main_pgs/issues/v10n2/Lugosi.pdf

Lyotard, J. (1979). *The postmodern condition: A report on knowledge.* In G. Bennington & B. Massumi (Trans.). Minneapolis, MN: University of Minnesota Press.

Marx, K. (2006a[1853]). The British rule in India. In I. Husain, I. Habib, & P. Patnaik (Eds.), *Karl Marx on India* (pp. 11–17). New Delhi, India: Tulika Books.

Marx, K. (2006b[1853]). The East India company- its history and results. In I. Husain, I. Habib & P. Patnaik (Eds.), *Karl Marx on India* (pp. 21–28). New Delhi, India: Tulika Books.

Marx, K. (2006c[1853]). The future results of British rule in India. In I. Husain, I. Habib & P. Patnaik (Eds.), *Karl Marx on India* (pp. 46–51). New Delhi, India: Tulika Books.

Mason, M. (2008). *The pirate's dilemma: How youth culture is reinventing capitalism.* New York, NY: Simon & Schuster.

McLaren, P., & Farahmandpur, R. (2002). Breaking signifying chains: A marxist position on postmodernism. In D. Hill, P. McLaren, M. Cole, & G. Rikowski (Eds.), *Marxism against postmodernism in educational theory* (pp. 35–66). Lanham, MD: Lexington Books.

117

REFERENCES

McLaren, P., & Jaramillo, N. (2007). *Pedagogy and praxis in the age of empire*. Rotterdam, The Netherlands: Sense.

Memmi, A. (1965). *The colonizer and the colonized*. Boston, MA: Beacon Press.

Morris, M. (2001). *Curriculum and the holocaust: Competing sights of memory and representation*. Mahweh, NJ: Lawrence Erlbaum Associates.

Moya, P. M. L. (2000). Postmodernism, realism, and the politics of identity. In P. M. L. Moya & M. R. Hames-Garcia (Eds.), *Reclaiming identity: Realist theory and the predicament of postmodernism* (pp. 67–101). Berkeley and Los Angeles: University of California Press.

Nandy, A. (1983). *The intimate enemy: Loss and recovery of self under colonialism*. New York, NY: Oxford University Press.

Nietzsche, F. (1967a). *On the geneology of morals*. In W. Kaufmann (Trans.). New York, NY: Vintage Books.

Nietzsche, F. (1967b). *The will to power*. In W. Kaufmann (Trans.). New York, NY: Random House.

Nietzsche, F. (2010[1886]). *Beyond good and evil*. In H. Zimmern (Trans.). Simon & Brown.

Ortega y Gasset, J. (1932). *The revolt of the masses*. New York, NY: Norton & Co.

Parry, D. (2006). *Blackbeard: The real pirate of the Caribbean*. New York, NY: Thunder's Mouth Press.

Peters, M. (2011). *The last book of postmodernism: Apocalyptic thinking, philosophy and education in the twenty-first century*. New York, NY: Peter Lang.

Pinar, W. F. (2004). *What is curriculum theory?*. Mahweh, NJ: Lawrence Erlbaum Associates.

Pinar, W., Reynolds, W., Slattery, P., & Taubman, P. (2004). *Understanding curriculum*. New York, NY: Peter Lang.

Purpel, D. E. (1999). *Moral outrage in education*. New York, NY: Peter Lang.

Ravitch, D. (2012, June 10). *Do not accept the new normal* (Website) (para 13). Retrieved October 7, 2012, from http://dianeravitch.net/2012/06/10/do-not-accept-the-new-normal/

Rediker, M. (1987). *Between the devil and the deep blue sea: Merchant seamen, pirates and the Anglo-American maritime world, 1700–1750*. New York, NY: Cambridge University Press.

Rikowski, G., & McLaren, P. (2002). Postmodernism in educational theory. In D. Hill, P. McLaren, M. Cole, & G. Rikowski (Eds.), *Marxism against postmodernism in educational theory* (pp. 3–13). Lanham, MD: Lexington Books.

Riley, C. (2012, June 26). *Top super PAC donors: The 9 largest super PAC donors have collectively donated over $60 million to various political causes. Who are these guys?* (Website). Retrieved September 3, 2012, from CNN Money: http://money.cnn.com/galleries/2012/news/economy/1206/gallery.super-pac-donors-politics/index.html

Robins, N. (2006). *The corporation that changed the world: How the East India Company shaped the modern multinational*. New York, NY: Pluto Press.

Said, E. W. (1979). *Orientalism*. New York, NY: Random House.

Said, E. W. (1993). *Culture and imperialism*. New York, NY: Vintage Books.

Said, E. W. (2007). *On orientalism* (Video File). Retrieved October 7, 2011, from http://www.youtube.com/watch?v=xwCOSkXR_Cw

Sanders, R. (2007). *If a pirate I must be: The true history of Black Bart, king of the Caribbean pirates*. New York, NY: Skyhorse Publishing.

Schlesinger, J. (2010, November 9). Cookiegate: Sarah Palin takes on 'nanny state' nutrition guidelines. *ABC News*. Retrieved July 8, 2011, from http://abcnews.go.com/blogs/politics/2010/11/sarah-palin-tackles-school-nutrition-debate-with-cookies/

Sewell, A. (2011, March 9). *Wisconsin republicans bypass democrats on union bill* (Website) (para 3). Retrieved April 23, 2012, from http://www.mcclatchydc.com/2011/03/09/110086/wisconsin-senate-gop-bypasses.html

Shiva, V. (2005). *Earth democracy: Justice, sustainability, and peace*. Cambridge, MA: South End Press.

Smith, A. (2003[1776]). *The wealth of nations*. New York, NY: Random House.

Smith, A. D., Smith, T. G., & Watkins, S. R. (2009). *The pop culture zone: Writing critically about popular culture*. Boston, MA: Wadsworth Cengage Learning.

Spivak, G. C. (1993). *Outside in the teaching machine*. New York, NY: Routledge.

Stanford, J. (2012, May 29). How ALEC gets real tax dollars for fake schools. In *Huffington post social reading* (Website) (para. 3). Retrieved September 3, 2012, from http://www.huffingtonpost.com/jason-stanford/alec-virtual-schools_b_1549202.html

Stevenson, R. L. (1993[1905]). *Treasure Island*. Mineola, NY: Dover Publications.

Stewart, J. (Host). (2011, February 28). Crisis in the dairy land: Angry Curds. In *The daily show with Jon Stewart* [Episode # 16029]. New York, NY: Comedy Central. (Video File). Retrieved from http://www.thedailyshow.com/watch/mon-february-28-2011/crisis-in-dairyland---angry-curds

Taubman, P. M. (2009). *Teaching by numbers: Deconstructing the discourse of standards and accountability in education*. New York, NY: Routledge.

The United States is the East India Company's endeavor. (2010). Video File. Retrieved October 9, 2011, from http://www.youtube.com/watch?v=O10ok7anPLE

Vallar, C. (2010). *Pirates and privateers: The history of maritime piracy* (Website). Retrieved May 18, 2011, from http://www.cindyvallar.com/GHP.html

Weaver, J. A., & Daspit, T. (2000). Critical pedagogy, popular culture and the creation of meaning. In T. Daspit & J. A. Weaver (Eds.), *Popular culture and critical pedagogy* (13–33). New York, NY and London, UK: Garland Publishing.

Wilson, P. L. (1995). *Pirate utopias; Moorish corsairs & European renegadoes* (2nd ed.). Brooklyn, NY: Autonomedia.

Printed in the United States
By Bookmasters